# Workshop on Computational Linguistics in a World of Social Media 2010



**Held at NAACL HLT 2010**

## Los Angeles, California, USA
## 6 June 2010

ISBN: 978-1-61738-674-9

**Printed from e-media with permission by:**

Curran Associates, Inc.
57 Morehouse Lane
Red Hook, NY 12571

CURRAN ASSOCIATES INC. proceedings.com

**Some format issues inherent in the e-media version may also appear in this print version.**



Printed by Curran Associates, Inc. (2010)



Association for Computational Linguistics
209 N. Eighth Street
Stroudsburg, Pennsylvania 18360

Phone: 1-570-476-8006
Fax: 1-570-476-0860

acl@aclweb.org

**Additional copies of this publication are available from:**

Curran Associates, Inc.
57 Morehouse Lane
Red Hook, NY 12571 USA
Phone: 845-758-0400
Fax: 845-758-2634
Email: curran@proceedings.com
Web: www.proceedings.com

# Introduction

Social Media eg Twitter, Blogs, Forums, FaceBook, Google Buzz has exploded over the last few years. FaceBook is now the most visited site in the US, overtaking Google in the first quarter of 2010. These sites contain the aggregated beliefs and opinions of millions of people on an epic range of topics, in a multitude of languages.

Social Media presents many challenges and opportunities to the ACL community, with this workshop being the first of its kind at a computational linguistics venue. Accepted papers range from story detection and tracking to discourse, applied across new and old media including company announcements, news, forums, blogs and micro-blogs. A notable aspect is the predominance of Twitter as a Social Media resource.

We experimented with a new kind of workshop based on a philosophy that ACL workshops should serve a different purpose than the main conference. To encourage submission of new ideas, we restricted papers to just two sides. And, to create a fast-paced and highly interactive workshop, each accepted paper was allotted a short talk and a poster.

Our invited talks touch upon various aspects of Social Media; distilling collective beliefs and making them concrete (Noah Smith); new technologies (Casey Whitelaw); the relationships between old and new media (Jochen Leidner). They give a balance between industry and academia and highlight the relationships between Human Language Technologies and Social Media.

We are grateful to Google Research for sponsoring the workshop. We used part of the sponsorship to award a prize to the best presentation (be it poster or short talk). This is a conscious decision to reward people for putting effort into communicating their ideas. At the time of writing this preface we have not made the award. But by the time you are reading this, it may well be you!

**Organizers:**

Ben Hachey, Capital Markets CRC and Macquarie University
Miles Osborne, University of Edinburgh

**Program Committee:**

Beatrice Alex, University of Edinburgh
Regina Barzilay, Massachusetts Institute of Technology
James Curran, University of Sydney
Murray Z. Frank, University of Minnesota
Michael Gamon, Microsoft Research
Nikesh Garera, Kosmix
Keith Hall, Google
John Henderson, MITRE
Bill Hu, Arkansas State University
Ben Hutchinson, Google
Rebecca Hwa, University of Pittsburgh
Mirella Lapata, University of Edinburgh
Victor Lavrenko, University of Edinburgh
Jochen Leidner, Thomson Reuters
Adam Lopez, University of Edinburgh
Craig Macaulay, Ernst & Young
Rob Malouf, San Diego State University
Yuval Marom, Pacific Brands
Rada Mihalcea, University of North Texas
Maria Milosavljevic, Macquarie University
Gabriel Murray, University of British Columbia
Deepak Ravichandran, Google
Calum Robertson, Sirca
Anoop Sarkar, Simon Fraser University
Robert P. Schumaker, Iona College
Noah Smith, Carnegie Mellon University
Tae Yano, Carnegie Mellon University

**Invited Speakers:**

Jochen Leidner, Thomson Reuters
Noah Smith, Carnegie Mellon University
Casey Whitelaw, Google

# Table of Contents

# Workshop Program

**Sunday, June 6, 2010**

**Session 1: Applications in Social Media**

| | |
|---|---|
| 9:00 | Invited Talk: *Text-Driven Forecasting*<br>Noah Smith, Carnegie Mellon University |
| 9:45 | *The "Nays" Have It: Exploring Effects of Sentiment in Collaborative Knowledge Sharing*<br>Ablimit Aji and Eugene Agichtein |
| 9:51 | *An Analysis of Verbs in Financial News Articles and their Impact on Stock Price*<br>Robert Schumaker |
| 9:57 | *Detecting Word Misuse in Chinese*<br>Wei Liu |
| 10:03 | *An Information-Retrieval Approach to Language Modeling: Applications to Social Data*<br>Juan Huerta |
| 10:09 | *Towards Automatic Question Answering over Social Media by Learning Question Equivalence Patterns*<br>Tianyong Hao, Wenyin Liu and Eugene Agichtein |
| 10:15 | Posters |
| 10:30 | Posters & Coffee |

**Sunday, June 6, 2010 (continued)**

**Session 2: Forums and Networks**



**Session 3: (Micro)-Blogs and Information Tracking**

**Sunday, June 6, 2010 (continued)**

14:33 *Labelling and Spatio-Temporal Grounding of News Events*
Bea Alex and Claire Grover

14:39 *Tracking Information Flow between Primary and Secondary News Sources*
Will Radford, Ben Hachey, James Curran and Maria Milosavljevic

14:45 *Detecting controversies in Twitter: a first study*
Marco Pennacchiotti and Ana-Maria Popescu

14:51 Posters

15:00 Posters & Coffee

16:00 Finish

# The "Nays" Have It: Exploring Effects of Sentiment in Collaborative Knowledge Sharing

**Ablimit Aji , Eugene Agichtein**
Mathematics & Computer Science Department
Emory University
{aaji,eugene}@mathcs.emory.edu

**Abstract**

In this paper we study what effects sentiment have on the temporal dynamics of user interaction and content generation in a knowledge sharing setting. We try to identify how sentiment influences interaction dynamics in terms of answer arrival, user ratings arrival, community agreement and content popularity. Our study suggests that "Negativity Bias" triggers more community attention and consequently more content contribution. Our findings provide insight into how users interact in online knowledge sharing communities, and helpful for improving existing systems.

## 1 Introduction

Recently, Collaborative Knowledge Sharing sites( or CQA sites), such as Naver and Yahoo! Answers have exploded in popularity. Already, for many information needs, these sites are becoming valuable alternatives to search engines. Previous studies identified visibility as an important factor for content popularity and developed models in static settings. However, when users post social media content, they might either explicitly or implicitly express their personal attitudes or sentiment. The following example illustrates a question with negative sentiment.

> $Q$ :*Obama keeps saying we need to sacrifice. What sacrifices has he and the gov made collectively and individually?*
> $A_1$: *Our hard earned tax dollars.* $17\uparrow, 2\downarrow$
> $A_2$: *None and they never will.* $18\uparrow, 2\downarrow$

Psychological studies (Smith et al., 2008) suggest that our brain has "Negativity Bias" - that is, people automatically devote more attention to negative information than to positive information. Thus, our attitudes may be more heavily influenced by negative opinions. Our hypothesis is that this kind of human cognitive bias would have measurable effects on how users respond to information need in CQA communities. Our goal in this paper is to understand how question sentiment influence the *dynamics* of the user interactions in CQA - that is, to understand how users respond to questions of different sentiment, how question sentiment affects community agreement on best answer and question popularity.

## 2 Sentiment Influence

While (Aji et al., 2010) suggests that question category has a patent influence on interaction dynamics, we mainly focus on sentiment in this exploratory study, for the reason that sentiment is a high level but prominent facet in every piece of content. We focused on how may sentiment effect the following dimensions:

- **Answer Arrival:** Measured as number of answers arrived every minute.
- **Vote Arrival:** Measured as number of votes arrived per answer.
- **Community Agreement:** Mean Reciprocal Rank (MRR), computed by ranking the answers in order of decreasing "Thumbs up" ratings, and identifying the rank of the actual "best" answer, as selected by the asker.

$$MRR = \frac{1}{|Q|}\sum_{i=1}^{N}\frac{1}{rank_i} \quad (1)$$

  where $rank_i$ is the rank of the best answer among the answers submitted for question $i$.
- **Answer Length, Question Length:** We examine whether questions with different sentiment exhibit variations in question and answer length.
- **Interest "Stars":** How many users marked question as interesting.

## 3 Dataset Description

For our study we tracked a total of approximately 10,000 questions, sampled from 20 categories from Yahoo! Answers. Specifically, each new question in our tracking list crawled every five minutes until it's closed. As a result, we obtained approximately 22



*Proceedings of the NAACL HLT 2010 Workshop on Computational Linguistics in a World of Social Media*, pages 1–2,
Los Angeles, California, June 2010. 

million question-answer-feedback snapshots in total. Since labeling all the questions would be expensive, we randomly selected 2000 questions from this dataset for human labeling. We then utilized the Amazon Mechanical Turk Service[1]. Five workers labeled each question as either *positive, negative or neutral*; the ratings were filtered by using majority opinion (at least 3 out of 5 labels). Overall statistics of this dataset are reported in Table 1. The overall inter-rater agreement was 65%.

| Positive | Negative | Neutral | Total |
|---|---|---|---|
| 379 | 173 | 548 | 1,100 |

Table 1: Statistics of the *Temporal* dataset

## 4 Results and Discussion

Figure 1 reports answer arrival dynamics for question with varying sentiment. Answers to negative questions arrive substantially faster than answers to positive or neutral questions, whereas the difference between positive and neutral questions are minor. This strongly confirms the "Negative Bias" effect. Given the fact that questions stay in the category front page relatively same amount of time where their visibility contributes potential answers, on average, negative sentiment questions managed to get more answers than two other types of questions (4.3 vs. 3.3 and 3.5). It seems, sentiment expressed in a question contributes to the answer arrival more than visibility.

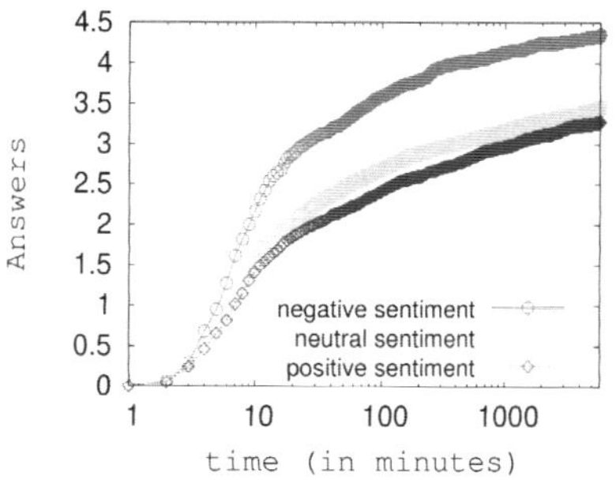


Figure 1: Cumulative answer arrival

Figure 2 reports rating arrival dynamics. Interestingly, positive *ratings* arrive much faster to negative questions, whereas positive and negative ratings arrive roughly at the same rate for positive and neutral questions. While this might be partially due to the fact that negative sentiment questions are more "attention grabbing" than other types of questions, we conjecture that this effect is caused by the selection bias of the raters participating in negative question threads, who tend to support answers that strongly

[1] http://www.mturk.com

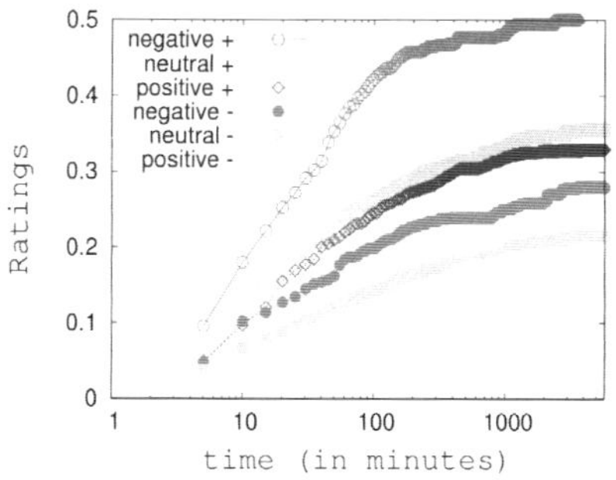


Figure 2: Cumulative user ratings arrival

agree (or strongly disagree) with the question asker. Surprisingly, community agreement(MRR) on the

| Type | MRR | QLength | ALength | Stars |
|---|---|---|---|---|
| Negative | 0.47 | **78** | 49 | **0.25** |
| Positive | 0.56 | 58 | **52** | 0.16 |
| Neutral | **0.57** | 52 | 47 | 0.15 |

Table 2: Agreement, Question length, Answer Length and Star count averaged over question type

best answer is lower for negative sentiment questions. On average, negative sentiment questions were marked as interesting more than positive or neutral questions were marked as interesting. Although this may sound counterintuitive, it is not surprising if we recall how the "Negative Bias" influences user behavior and may increase implicit "visibility". All the above mentioned differences are statistically significant(t-test $p = 0.05$).

In summary, our preliminary exploration indicates that sentiment may have a powerful effect on the content contribution dynamics in collaborative question answering, and is a promising direction for further study of knowledge sharing communities.

## Acknowledgments

We thank HP Social Computing Labs for support.

## References

Ablimit Aji. Eugene Agichtein. 2010. *Deconstructing Interaction Dynamics in Knowledge Sharing Communities.* International Conference on Social Computing, Behavioral Modeling, & Prediction.

Gabor Szabo. Bernardo Huberman. 2008. *Predicting the popularity of online content.* HP Labs Technical Report.

Kristina Lerman. 2007. *Social Information Processing in Social News Aggregation.* IEEE Internet Computing: Special Issue on Social Search.

N. Kyle Smith Jeff T. Larsen Tanya L. Chartrand John T. Cacioppo 2006. *Affective Context Moderates the Attention Bias Toward Negative Information.* Journal of Personality and Social Psychology.

# An Analysis of Verbs in Financial News Articles and their Impact on Stock Price

**Robert P. Schumaker**
Iona College
715 North Ave
New Rochelle, NY 10801, USA
rob.schumaker@gmail.com

## Abstract

Article terms can move stock prices. By analyzing verbs in financial news articles and coupling their usage with a discrete machine learning algorithm tied to stock price movement, we can build a model of price movement based upon the verbs used, to not only identify those terms that can move a stock price the most, but also whether they move the predicted price up or down.

## 1 Introduction

Predicting market movements is a difficult problem that deals mostly with trying to model human behavior. However, with the advent of quantitative trading systems its now easier to dissect their trading decisions. These systems are nearly instantaneous in their ability to make trades, but their Achilles heel is a reliance on human counterparts to translate relevant news into numeric data. This introduces a serious lag-time in trading decisions.

## 2 Literature Review

Information is fed into the market all the time. While some information sources can move a stock price, e.g., rumors and scandals; financial news articles are considered more stable and a form of its own commodity (Mowshowitz, 1992).

The first challenge of a textual financial prediction system is to manage the large amounts of textual information that exist for securities such as periodic SEC filings, press releases and financial news articles. These textual documents can then be parsed using Natural Language Processing (NLP) techniques to identify specific article terms most likely to cause share price changes. By automating this process, machines can take advantage of arbitrage opportunities faster than human counterparts by repeatedly forecasting price fluctuations and executing immediate trades.

Once financial news articles have been gathered, we need to represent their important features in machine-friendly form. We chose to implement a verb representation scheme which was found to be most predictive for financial news articles.

Assigning a representational mechanism is not sufficient to address scalability issues associated with large datasets. A common solution is to introduce a term frequency threshold (Joachims, 1998). This technique not only eliminates noise from lesser used terms, but also reduces the number of features to represent. Once scalability issues have been addressed, the data needs to be prepared in a more machine-friendly manner. One popular method is to represent article terms in binary where the term is either present or not in a given article. This solution leads to large but sparse matrices where the number of represented terms throughout the dataset will greatly outnumber the terms used in an individual article.

Once financial news articles have been represented, learning algorithms can then begin to identify patterns of predictable behavior. One ac-



*Proceedings of the NAACL HLT 2010 Workshop on Computational Linguistics in a World of Social Media*, pages 3–4,
Los Angeles, California, June 2010. 

cepted method, Support Vector Regression (SVR), is a regression equivalent of Support Vector Machines (SVM) but without the aspect of classification. This method is also well-suited to handling textual input as binary representations and has been used in similar financial news studies (Schumaker & Chen, 2006; Tay & Cao, 2001).

## 3 System Design

To analyze our data, we constructed the AZFinText system. The numeric component gathers price data in one minute increments from a stock price database. The textual piece gathers financial news articles from Yahoo! Finance and represents them by their verbs.

For the machine learning algorithm we chose to implement the SVR Sequential Minimal Optimization function through Weka. This function allows discrete numeric prediction instead of classification. We selected a linear kernel and ten-fold cross-validation.

## 4 Experimental Design

For the experiment, we selected a consecutive five week period of time to serve as our experimental baseline. This period of research from Oct. 26, 2005 to Nov. 28, 2005 was selected because it did not have unusual market conditions and was a good testbed for our evaluation. We further limited our scope of activity to only those companies listed in the S&P 500 as of Oct. 3, 2005. Articles gathered during this period were restricted to occur between the hours of 10:30am and 3:40pm. A further constraint to reduce the effects of confounding variables was introduced where two articles on the same company cannot exist within twenty minutes of each other or both will be discarded. The above processes filtered the 9,211 candidate news articles gathered during this period to 2,802, and 10,259,042 stock quotations.

The first task is to extract financial news articles. The entire corpus of financial news articles are represented by their verbs in binary. If a particular verb is present in the article, that feature is given a 1, else a 0 and then stored in the database. To build a model, we first pair together the representational verb and stock quotation at the time the article was released, for each financial news article. This data is then passed to the SVR algorithm where a multi-dimensional price prediction model is constructed. This weighted model can then be dissected to determine the most relevant factors that can influence price movement.

## 5 Results and Discussion

From the trained AZFinText system, it was unsurprising that a majority of weight was placed on the stock price at the time the article was released and is consistent with prior observation where the article terms were found to be important and were used to fine-tune price prediction. Of the verbs, 211 were used by the system as support vectors. An abbreviated multi-dimensional price prediction model is as follows. The constants represent the weight given by the SVR algorithm and the verbs are binary, representing their existence within the financial news article.

$$0.9997\text{Intial\_Price} + 0.0045\textit{planted} + 0.004\textit{announcing} + 0.003\textit{front} + 0.0029\textit{smaller} + 0.0028\textit{crude} - 0.0029\textit{hereto} - 0.002\textit{comparable} - 0.0018\textit{charge} - 0.0015\textit{summit} - 0.0015\textit{green}$$

The five verbs with highest negative impact on stock price are *hereto*, *comparable*, *charge*, *summit* and green. If the verb *hereto* were to appear in a financial article, AZFinText would discount the price by $0.0029. While this movement may not appear to be much, the continued usage of negative verbs is additive.

The five verbs with the highest positive impact on stock prices are *planted*, *announcing*, *front*, *smaller* and *crude*.

## References


Joachims, T. 1998. Text Categorization with Support Vector Machines: Learning with Many Relevant Features. *European Conference on Machine Learning*, Chemnitz, Germany.

Mowshowitz, A. 1992. On the Market Value of Information Commodities. The Nature of Information and Information Commodities. *Journal of the American Society for Information Science* 43(3): 225-232.

Schumaker, R. P. & H. Chen 2006. Textual Analysis of Stock Market Prediction Using Financial News Articles. *Americas Conference on Information Systems*, Acapulco, Mexico.

Tay, F. & L. Cao 2001. Application of Support Vector Machines in Financial Time Series Forecasting. *Omega* 29: 309-317.

# Detecting Word Misuse in Chinese

**Wei Liu**
Department of Computer Science
University of Sheffield
W.Liu@dcs.shef.ac.uk

## Abstract

Social Network Service (SNS) and personal blogs have become the most popular platform for online communication and sharing information. However because most modern computer keyboards are Latin-based, Asian language speakers (such as Chinese) has to rely on a input system which accepts Romanisation of the characters and convert them into characters or words in that language. In Chinese this form of Romanisation (usually called Pinyin) is highly ambiguous, word misuses often occur because the user choose a wrong candidate or deliveratelly substitute the word with another character string that has the identical Romanisation to convey certain semantics, or to achieve a sarcasm effect. In this paper we aim to develop a system that can automatically identify such word misuse, and suggest the correct word to be used.

## 1 Introduction

A certain kind of derogatory opinion is being conveyed in Chinese chat forums and SNS sites through the use of Chinese Hanzi (hieroglyphic) characters. There is potential for this to happen whenever two expressions are pronounced in a similar way in Chinese. For exmaple, irate readers have used "妓者" ("Ji Zhe") for "记者" ("Ji Zhe"). While "记者" means reporter or journalist, "妓者" can be interpreted as prostitute.

There are 5000 commonly used characters. While the number of distinct Pinyin (toneless) is only 412. Therefore Pinyin to character conversion is highly ambigurous and is a active research topic (Zhou et al., 2007), (Lin and Zhang, 2008), (Chen and Lee, 2000). On the other hand, automatic Pinyin generation is considered a solved task, (Liu and Guthrie, 2009) shows that using the most frequent Pinyin approach to assign Pinyin to each character can achieve 98% accuracy. In fact, we test on the Gigaword Chinese (Verson 2) corpus and find out that only about 15% of the characters have ambigurous Pinyin.

## 2 Automatically Detecting Word Misuse

We divided the detection process into three steps as below:

- Segmentation: Given a piece of Chinese text, we first feed it into an automatic word segmenter (Zhang et al., 2003) to break the text into semantic units. Because we consider only multiple-character anomaly cases, anomalies can only be contained within sequences of single characters.
- Character sequence extraction: After segmentation, we are interested in sequences of single characters, because anomalies will occur only within those sequences. Once we obtain these sequences, we generate all possible substrings for each sequence because any anomalous words can be part of a character sequence.
- Detection: We assume the anomaly shares many phonetic similarities with the "true" word. As a result we need a method for comparing pronunciations of two character sequences. Here we use the Pinyin to represent phonetics of a Chinese character, and we define two pronunciations to be similar when they both have identical Pinyin (not including the tone). We use character-to-pinyin conversion tool[1] to create a Pinyin-to-Word hash table using the machine-segmented Chinese Gigaword

[1] http://pinyin4j.sourceforge.net/



*Proceedings of the NAACL HLT 2010 Workshop on Computational Linguistics in a World of Social Media*, pages 5–6,
Los Angeles, California, June 2010. 

ver. 2. Once we have the resources, we first produce all possible Pinyin sequences of each character sequence.Next we do a Pinyin-word look up in the hash table we created; if there exists any entries, we know that the Pinyin sequence maps to one or more 'real' words. Consequently, we consider any character sequences whose Pinyin maps to these words to be possible anomalies.

## 3 Data and Experiments

We have conducted preliminary experiments to test our algorithm. To start with, we manually gathered a small number of documents which contain anomalous phrases of the type described above. The documents are gathered from internet chat-rooms and contain 3,797 Chinese characters: the anomalies herein are shown in table 1.

| Intended word | Misused character seq. | Pinyin | Freq |
|---|---|---|---|
| 美国 (The U.S.) | 霉国 | Mei guo | 43 |
| 教授 (Professor) | 叫兽 | Jiao shou | 23 |
| 偶像 (Role model) | 呕像or 呕象 | Ou xiang | 12 |

Table 1: Testing document

### 3.1 Results and Discussions

We evaluate our identification/correction performance using standard measures of standard precision and recall. We tested our performance using bigram thresholds of 0, 1 and 2.

Table 2 shows the performances of our method.

| | |
|---|---|
| No. of misused chararcter sequence | 78 |
| Total identified | 130 |
| Correctly identified | 78 |
| Precision | 60% |
| Recall | 100% |
| F-measure | 75% |

Table 2: Result for word misuse identification

The initial experiments showed that our method can successfully identify and correct the three examples of non-word anomalies with reasonable precision and recall. The method obtains 100% recall however it generates a lot of false positives; this can be seen in a relatively low precision of 60%.

In summary, our method is successful at identifying genuine anomalous non-word character sequences; however the method also retrieves some false positives, due to the highly ambiguous Pinyin to word mappings.

## 4 Future Work

Our experiments shows that our preliminary method can detect word misuses due to the Pinyin sequence being idential but with a relatively high false positives. In the future we plan to use other contextual evidence, such as pointwise mutual information to model whether the candidate sequence generated by our method is a better fit than the original sequence. We also plan to gather more real data that contain misuse of our interests.

## References


Chen, Z. and Lee, K.-F. (2000). A new statistical approach to chinese pinyin input. In *In Proceedings of the 38th Annual Meeting on Association for Computational Linguistics*, pages 241–247, Hong Kong.

Lin, B. and Zhang, J. (2008). A novel statistical chinese language model and its application in pinyin-to-character conversion. In *CIKM '08: Proceeding of the 17th ACM conference on Information and knowledge management*, pages 1433–1434, New York, NY, USA. ACM.

Liu, W. and Guthrie, L. (2009). Chinese pinyin-text conversion on segmented text. In *TSD '09: Proceedings of the 12th International Conference on Text, Speech and Dialogue*, pages 116–123, Berlin, Heidelberg. Springer-Verlag.

Zhang, H.-P., Liu, Q., Cheng, X.-Q., Zhang, H., and Yu, H.-K. (2003). Chinese lexical analysis using hierarchical hidden markov model. In *Proceedings of the second SIGHAN workshop on Chinese language processing*, pages 63–70, Morristown, NJ, USA. Association for Computational Linguistics.

Zhou, X., Hu, X., Zhang, X., and Shen, X. (2007). A segment-based hidden markov model for real-setting pinyin-to-chinese conversion. In *CIKM '07: Proceedings of the sixteenth ACM conference on Conference on information and knowledge management*, pages 1027–1030, New York, NY, USA. ACM.

# An Information-Retrieval Approach to Language Modeling: Applications to Social Data

**Juan M. Huerta**
IBM T. J.Watson Research Center
1101 Kitchawan Road
Yorktown Heights, NY 10598, USA
huerta@us.ibm.com

### Abstract

In this paper we propose the IR-LM (Information Retrieval Language Model) which is an approach to carrying out language modeling based on large volumes of constantly changing data as is the case of social media data. Our approach addresses specific characteristics of social data: large volume of constantly generated content as well as the need to frequently integrating and removing data from the model.

## 1 Introduction

We describe the Information Retrieval Language Model (IR-LM) which is a novel approach to language modeling motivated by domains with constantly changing large volumes of linguistic data. Our approach is based on information retrieval methods and constitutes a departure from the traditional statistical n-gram language modeling (SLM) approach. We believe the IR-LM is more adequate than SLM when: (a) language models need to be updated constantly, (b) very large volumes of data are constantly being generated and (c) it is possible and likely that the sentence we are trying to score has been observed in the data (albeit with small possible variations). These three characteristics are inherent of social domains such as blogging and micro-blogging.

## 2 N-gram SLM and IR-LM

Statistical language models are widely used in main computational linguistics tasks to compute the probability of a string of words: $p(w_1...w_i)$

To facilitate its computation, this probability is expressed as:

$$p(w_1...w_i) = P(w_1) \times P(w_2 \mid w_1) \times ... \times P(w_i \mid w_1...w_{i-1})$$

Assuming that only the most immediate word history affects the probability of any given word, and focusing on a trigram language model:

$$P(w_i \mid w_1...w_{i-1}) \approx P(w_i \mid w_{i-2} w_{i-1})$$

This leads to:

$$P(w_1...w_i) \approx \prod_{k=1..i} p(w_k \mid w_{k-1} w_{k-2})$$

Language models are typically applied in ASR, MT and other tasks in which multiple hypotheses need to be rescored according to their likelihood (i.e., ranked). In a smoothed backoff SLM (e.g., Goodman (2001)), all the n-grams up to order n are computed and smoothed and backoff probabilities are calculated. If new data is introduced or removed from the corpus, the whole model, the counts and weights would need to be recalculated. Levenberg and Osborne (2009) proposed an approach for incorporating new data as it is seen in the stream. Language models have been used to support IR as a method to extend queries (Lavrenko et al. 2001); in this paper we focus on using IR to carry out language modeling.

### 2.1 The IR Language Model

The IR-LM approach consists of two steps: the first is the identification of a set of matches from a corpus given a query sentence, and second is the estimation of a likelihood-like value for the query.

In the first step, given a corpus *C* and a query sentence *S,* we identify the k-closest matching sentences in the corpus through an information retrieval approach. We propose the use of a modified String Edit Distance as score in the IR process. To efficiently carry out the search of the closest sentences in the corpus we propose the use of an inverted index with word position



*Proceedings of the NAACL HLT 2010 Workshop on Computational Linguistics in a World of Social Media*, pages 7–8,
Los Angeles, California, June 2010. 

information and a stack based search approach described in Huerta (2010). A modification of the SED allows queries to match portions of long sentences (considering local insertion deletions and substitutions) without penalizing for missing the non-local portion of the matching sentence.

In the second step, in general, we would like to compute a likelihood-like value of $S$ through a function of the distances (or alternatively, similarity scores) of the query $S$ to the top k-hypotheses. However, for now we will focus on the more particular problem of ranking multiple sentences in order of matching scores, which, while not directly producing likelihood estimates it will allow us to implement n-best rescoring. Specifically, our ranking is based on the level of matching between each sentence to be ranked and its best matching hypothesis in the corpus. In this case, integrating and removing data from the model simply involve adding to or pruning the index which generally are simpler than n-gram re-estimation.

There is an important fundamental difference between the classic n-gram SLM approach and our approach. The n-gram approach says that a sentence $S_1$ is more likely than another sentence $S_2$ given a model if the n-grams that constitute $S_1$ have been observed more times than the n-grams of $S_2$. Our approach, on the other hand, says that a sentence $S_1$ is more likely than $S_2$ if the closest match to $S_1$ in $C$ resembles $S_1$ better than the closes match of $S_2$ resembles $S_2$ regardless of how many times these sentences have been observed.

## 3 Experiments

We carried out experiments using the blog corpus provided by Spinn3r (Burton et al (2009)). It consists of 44 million blog posts that originated during August and September 2008 from which we selected, cleaned, normalized and segmented 2 million English language blogs. We reserved the segments originating from blogs dated September 30 for testing.

We took 1000 segments from the test subset and for each of these segments we built a 16-hypothesis cohort (by creating 16 overlapping sub-segments of the constant length from the segment).

We built a 5-gram SLM using a 20k word dictionary and Knesser-Ney smoothing using the SRILM toolkit (Stolcke (2002)). We then ranked each of the 1000 test cohorts using each of the model's n-gram levels (unigram, bigram, etc.). Our goal is to determine to what extent our approach correlates with an n-gram SLM-based rescoring.

For testing purposes we re-ranked each of the test cohorts using the IR-LM approach. We then compared the rankings produced by n-grams and by IR-LM for every n-gram order and several IR configurations. For this, we computed the Spearman rank correlation coefficient (SRCC). SRCC averages for each configuration are shown in table 1. Row 1 shows the SRCC for the best overall IR configuration and row 2 shows the SRCC for the IR configuration producing the best results for each particular n-gram model. We can see that albeit simple, IR-LM can produce results consistent with a language model based on fundamentally different assumptions.

| | n=1 | n=2 | n=3 | n=4 | n=5 |
|---|---|---|---|---|---|
| overall | 0.53 | 0.42 | 0.40 | 0.40 | 0.38 |
| individual | 0.68 | 0.47 | 0.40 | 0.40 | 0.39 |

**Table 1.** Spearman rank correlation coefficient for several n-gram IR configurations

## 4 Conclusion

The IR-LM can be beneficial when the language model needs to be updated with added and removed data. This is particularly important in social data where new content is constantly generated. Our approach also introduces a different interpretation of the concept of likelihood of a sentence: instead of assuming the frequentist assumption underlying n-gram models, it is based on sentence feasibility based on the closest segment similarity. Future work will look into: integrating information from the top k-matches, likelihood regression, as well as leveraging other approaches to information retrieval.

## References


Burton K., Java A., and Soboroff I. (2009) The ICWSM 2009 Spinn3r Dataset. *Proc. ICWSM 2009*

Goodman J. (2001) A Bit of Progress in Language Modeling, *MS Res. Tech. Rpt. MSR-TR-2001-72.*

Huerta J. (2010) A Stack Decoder Approach to Approximate String Matching, *Proc. of SIGIR 2010*

Lavrenko V. and Croft W. B. (2001) Relevance based language models. *Proc. of SIGIR 2001*

Levenberg A. and Osborne M. (2009), Stream-based Randomised Lang. Models for SMT, *EMNLP 2009*

Stolcke A. (2002)s SRILM -- An Extensible Language Modeling Toolkit. *Proc. ICSLP 2002*

# Towards Automatic Question Answering over Social Media by Learning Question Equivalence Patterns

**Tianyong Hao**[1]
City University of Hong Kong
81 Tat Chee Avenue
Kowloon, Hong Kong SAR
haotianyong@gmail.com

**Wenyin Liu**
City University of Hong Kong
81 Tat Chee Avenue
Kowloon, Hong Kong SAR
csliuwy@cityu.edu.hk

**Eugene Agichtein**
Emory University
201 Dowman Drive
Atlanta, Georgia 30322 USA
eugene@mathcs.emory.edu

## Abstract

Many questions submitted to Collaborative Question Answering (CQA) sites have been answered before. We propose an approach to automatically generating an answer to such questions based on automatically learning to identify "equivalent" questions. Our main contribution is *an unsupervised method for automatically learning question equivalence patterns from CQA archive data*. These patterns can be used to match new questions to their equivalents that have been answered before, and thereby help suggest answers automatically. We experimented with our method approach over a large collection of more than 200,000 real questions drawn from the Yahoo! Answers archive, automatically acquiring over 300 groups of question equivalence patterns. These patterns allow our method to obtain over 66% precision on automatically suggesting answers to new questions, significantly outperforming conventional baseline approaches to question matching.

## 1 Introduction

Social media in general exhibit a rich variety of information sources. Question answering (QA) has been particularly amenable to social media, as it allows a potentially more effective alternative to web search by directly connecting users with the information needs to users willing to share the information directly (Bian, 2008). One of the useful by-products of this process is the resulting large archives of data – which in turn could be good sources of information for automatic question answering. Yahoo! Answers, as a collaborative QA system (CQA), has acquired an archive of more than 40 Million Questions and 500 Million answers, as of 2008 estimates.

The main premise of this paper is that there are many questions that are syntactically different while semantically similar. The key problem is how to identify such question groups. Our method is based on the key observation that *when the best non-trivial answers chosen by asker in the same domain are exactly the same, the corresponding questions are semantically similar*. Based on this observation, we propose answering new method for learning question equivalence patterns from CQA archives. First, we retrieve "equivalent" question groups from a large dataset by grouping them by the text of the best answers (as chosen by the askers). The equivalence patterns are then generated by learning common syntactic and lexical patterns for each group. To avoid generating patterns from questions that were grouped together by chance, we estimate the group's *topic diversity* to filter the candidate patterns. These equivalence patterns are then compared against newly submitted questions. In case of a match, the new question can be answered by proposing the "best" answer from a previously answered equivalent question.

We performed large-scale experiments over a more than 200,000 questions from Yahoo! Answers. Our method generated over 900 equivalence patterns in 339 groups and allows to correctly suggest an answer to a new question, roughly 70% of the time – outperforming conventional similarity-based baselines for answer suggestion.

Moreover, for the newly submitted questions, our method can identify equivalent questions and generate equivalent patterns incrementally, which can greatly improve the feasibility of our method.

## 2 Learning Equivalence Patterns

While most questions that share exactly the same "best" answer are indeed semantically equivalent, some may share the same answer by chance. To

[1] Work done while visiting Emory University



*Proceedings of the NAACL HLT 2010 Workshop on Computational Linguistics in a World of Social Media*, pages 9–10,
Los Angeles, California, June 2010. ©2010 Association for Computational Linguistics

filter out such cases, we propose an estimate of Topical Diversity (TD), calculated based on the shared topics for all pairs of questions in the group. If the diversity is larger than a threshold, the questions in this group are considered *not* equivalent, and no patterns are generated. To calculate this measure, we consider as topics the "notional words" (NW) in the question, which are the head nouns and the heads of verb phrases recognized by the OpenNLP parser. Using these words as "topics", *TD* for a group of questions *G* is calculated as:

$$TD(G) = \frac{2}{n(n-1)} \times \sum_{i=1}^{n-1} \sum_{j=2}^{n} \left(1 - \frac{Q_i \cap Q_j}{Q_i \cup Q_j}\right) \quad (i < j)$$

where $Q_i$ and $Q_j$ are the notional words in each question in within group *G* with n questions total.

Based on the question groups, we can generate equivalence patterns to extend the matching coverage – thus retrieving similar questions with different syntactic structure. OpenNLP is used to generate the basic syntactic structures by phrase chunking. After that, only the chunks which contain NWs are analyzed to acquire the phrase labels as the syntactic pattern. Table 1 shows an example of a generated pattern.

| |
|---|
| **Question**: What was the first book you discovered that made you think reading wasn't a complete waste of time?<br>**Pattern**: [NP]-[VP]-[NP]-[NP]-[VP]-[VP]-[NP]-[VP]-...<br>**NW**: (**Disjoint**: read waste time) (**Shared**: book think) |
| **Question**: What book do you think everyone should have at home?<br>**Pattern**: [NP]-[NP]-[VP]-[NP]-[VP]-[PP]-[NP]<br>**NW**: (**Disjoint**: do everyone have home) (**Shared**: book think) |

Table 1. A group of equivalence patterns

## 3 Experimental Evaluation

Our dataset is 216,563 questions and 2,044,296 answers crawled from Yahoo! Answers. From this we acquired 833 groups of similar questions distributed in 65 categories. After filtering by topical diversity, 339 groups remain to generate equivalence patterns. These groups contain 979 questions, with, 2.89 questions per group on average.

After that, we split our data into 413 questions for training (200 groups) and 566 questions, with randomly selected an additional 10,000 questions, for testing (the remainder) to compare three variants of our system Equivalence patterns only (EP), Notional words only (NW), and the weighted combination (EP+NW). To match question, both equivalence patterns and notional words are used with different weights. The weight of pattern, disjoint NW and shared NW are 0.7, 0.4 and 0.6 after parameter training. We then compare the variants and results are reported in Table 2, showing that EP+NW achieves the highest performance.

| | Recall | Precision | F1 score |
|---|---|---|---|
| EP | 0.811 | 0.385 | 0.522 |
| NW | 0.378 | 0.559 | 0.451 |
| EP+NW | 0.726 | 0.663 | 0.693 |

Table 2. Performance comparison of three variants

Using EP+NW as our best method, we now compare it to traditional similarity-based methods on whole question set. TF*IDF-based vector space model (TFIDF), and a more highly tuned Cosine model (that only keeps the same "notional words" filtered by phrase chunking) are used as baselines. Figure 3 reports the results, which indicate that EP+NW, outperforms both Cosine and TFIDF methods on all metrics.

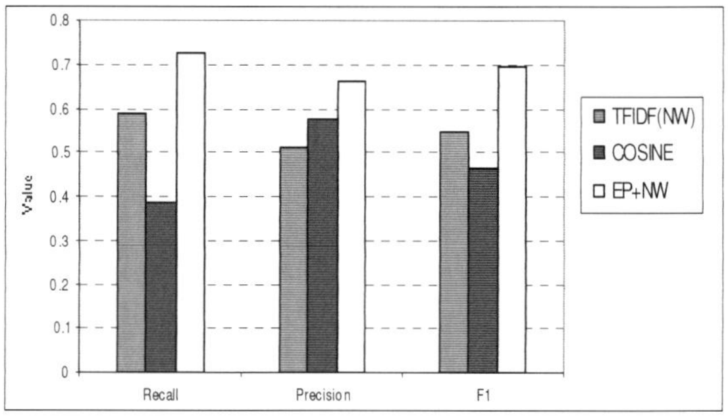


Figure 3. Performance of EP+NW vs. baselines

Our work expands on previous significant efforts on CQA retrieval (e.g., Bian et al., Jeon et al., Kosseim et al.). Our contribution is a new unsupervised and effective method for learning question equivalence patterns that exploits the structure of the collaborative question answering archives – an important part of social media.

## 4 References

Bian, J., Liu, Y., Agichtein, E., and Zha, H. 2008. *Finding the right facts in the crowd: factoid question answering over social media*. WWW.

Jeon, J., Croft, B.W. and Lee, J.H. 2005. *Finding similar questions in large question and answer archives Export Find Similar*. CIKM.

Kosseim, L. and Yousefi, J. 2008.*Improving the performance of question answering with semantically equivalent answer patterns*, Journal of Data & Knowledge Engineering.

# Modeling Message Roles and Influence in Q&A Forums

**Jeonhyung Kang and Jihie Kim**
University of Southern California
Information Sciences Institute
4676 Admiralty Was, Marina del Rey, CA, U.S.A
{jeonhyuk, jihie}@isi.edu

**Abstract**

We are modeling roles of individual messages and participants in Q&A discussion forums. In this paper, we present a mixed network model that represents message exchanges and message influences within a discussion thread. We first model individual message roles and thread-level user roles using discussion content features. We then combine the resulting message roles and the user roles to generate the overall influence network. Message influences and their aggregation over the network are analyzed using B-centrality measures. We use the results in identifying the most influential message in answering the initial question of the thread.

## 1 Introduction

Online discussion boards play an important role in various fields, including science, politics, and education. Understanding patterns of group interactions can be important in many applications. For example, in Q&A forums, some messages contain more useful or influential answers than others. Identifying useful content can help future discussions with similar issues. That is, useful information on a topic can be sent to related discussions (Kim et al., 2009).

There has been some work on analyzing dialogue patterns in online discussion boards (Feng et al, 2006). Some of these model message roles using dialogue acts such as question act or answer act. Most of these focus on modeling individual messages, often using surface forms. There has been limited study on thread-level modeling of the true roles of the messages, whether they provide information (*source*) or seek information (*sink*), or which message in the thread is most useful or influential as the source.

In this paper, we present a novel model of message influence within a discussion thread. In modeling the thread-level influence of the messages, besides the sink/source role of the individual messages, we take into account the roles of the message posters within the thread. In Q&A discussion threads, since the roles of the posters as an information provider or an information seeker often do not change within the same thread, such information can help us identify the true roles or influence of the messages.

We combine the message roles and the user roles with a network model. Message influences and their aggregation over the network are analyzed using B-centrality measures. We use the resulting influence scores in identifying the most influential message in answering the initial question of the thread.

## 2 Modeling Message Influence

We use discussion data from an Operating Systems course in the Computer Science department at the University of Southern California. Students use a discussion board, most commonly, to seek help on the project assignments. For this study, we use data from the Fall 2007 semester, with 177 discussion threads (randomly choose 133 for training and 44 for test) with 580 messages (randomly choose 451 for training and 129 for test).

### 2.1 Sink and source roles of a message

For each pair of messages where one is a reply to the other, we model the roles of the latter, as a *sink* or a *source* with respect to the former message or the message author. Some messages, especially long ones, can have both roles. Figure 1 shows an influence model of sink and source. A node represents either a user or a message. An edge is either a reply-to relation between two messages or an ownership of a message by a user. The direction of each edge indicates the direction of influence. A source is a message that provides information and it generates influence. In the top graph, B responds



*Proceedings of the NAACL HLT 2010 Workshop on Computational Linguistics in a World of Social Media*, pages 11–12,
Los Angeles, California, June 2010. 

to A's message as an information source. A sink message requests information from others so the edge direction goes towards it. Note that sinks and sources are different from questions and answers since some of sources can take a form of a question (e.g. have you checked the manual?).

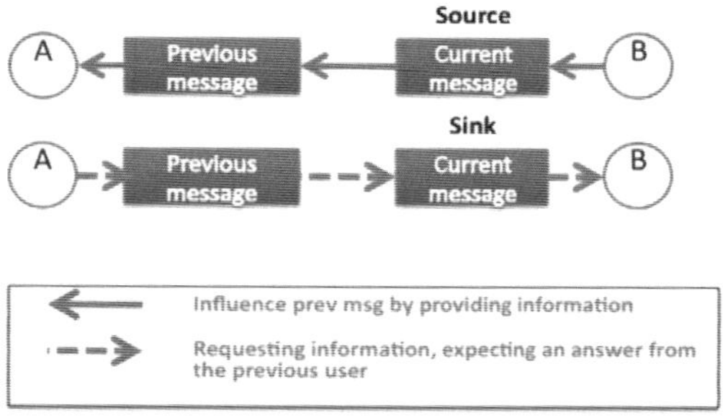


Figure 1: Sink and source role of a message

### 2.2 Information seeker and information provider: Thread level roles

Figure 2 shows an influence model of an information seeker and an information provider when they exchange messages. The information flows from the information provider to the information seeker, as indicated by the direction of the edges. In general, the initial poster seeks information and his or her role does not usually change within the thread. Without loss of generality, we assume that within a discussion thread, a user's role doesn't change for a certain amount of time, although he or she can post both Sink and Source messages, as shown in Figure 2. Using this model, we can capture the intention of the message based on who posted the message.

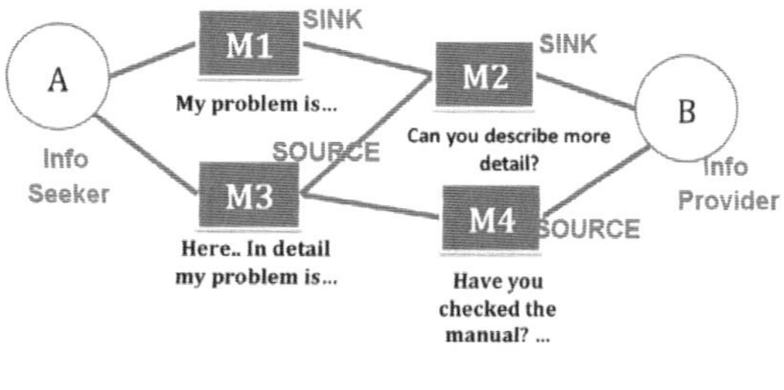


Figure 2: Thread-level user intention and message roles

### 2.3 Message and Participant Role Classifiers

Individual messages were annotated with sink and source information. The same message can have both sink and source roles with respect to the prior message or its poster.

The features used include cue phases (n-grams) and their positions, message position in the thread, author change information, the relative position of the message in the thread, a user's participation frequency (normalized), n-gram of previous messages with their positions and the message length. The details of these features are described in Kim et al (2009).

We used a Support Vector Machine (Chang and Lin 2001) to create two binary classifiers (since one message can have both roles) that identify message roles: source and sink, and one binary classifier for user roles: *information seeker and information provider*. The precisions/recalls range from 0.89 to 0.96. F-scores are within 0.92-0.93.

## 3 Profiling Influence of Message with Centrality Measures

We generate a message-role graph and a user-role graph using the above model, and generate influence network combining user and message roles. Message influences and their aggregation over the network are analyzed using B-centrality measures. To evaluate our source score accuracy (Ghosh and Lerman 2009), we annotated the most influential source message for the initial question (sink) in each thread. We use Mean Reciprocal Rank Score (MRR) to evaluate our results. The combined model provides better results with an MRR score of 0.90.

| Ranking strategy | Information used | MRR |
|---|---|---|
| ***Influence Network Model score*** | **User role + msg role** | **0.90** |
| *Earlier source msg* | **msg role** + msg location | 0.74 |
| *Earlier msg from info providers* | **User role** + msg location | 0.68 |

Table 2: MRR scores for different strategies

## Acknowledgement

This work was supported by National Science Foundation, CCLI Phase II (#0618859).

## References

Feng, D. Shaw, E. Kim, J. and Hovy, E. An Intelligent Discussion-Bot for Answering Student Queries in Threaded Discussions, Proc. of *IUI-2006*.

Ghosh, R. and Lerman, K. The structure of heterogeneous networks. Proc. of *IEEE Social Comp. Conf. 2009*.

Kim, J., Li, J., and Kim, T. Identifying student online discussions with unanswered questions,Proc. K-CAP 2009.

# Towards Modeling Social and Content Dynamics in Discussion Forums

**Jihie Kim and Aram Galstyan**
Information Sciences Institute / Univesity of Southern California
Marina del Rey, CA, USA
{jihie,galstyan}@isi.edu

## Extended Abstract

Recent years have witnessed the transformation of the World Wide Web from an information-gathering and processing tool into an interactive communication medium in the form of online discussion forums, chat–rooms, blogs, and so on. There is strong evidence suggesting that social networks facilitate new ways to interact with information in such media. Understanding the mechanisms and the patterns of such interactions can be important for many applications. Currently, there is not much work that adequately models interaction between social networks and information content. From the perspective of social network analysis, most existing work is concerned with understanding static topological properties of social networks represented by such forums. For instance, Park and Maurer (2009) applied node clustering to identify consensus and consensus facilitators, while Kang et al. (2009) uses discussion thread co-participation relations to identify (static) groups in discussions. On discussion content analysis research side, there have been approaches for classifying messages with respect to dialogue roles (Carvalho and Cohen, 2005; Ravi and Kim, 2007), but they often ignore the role and the impact of underlying social interactions.

Thus, the current static network and content analysis approaches provide limited support for

- Capturing dynamics of social interactions: the sequence of communication or who is responding to whom is important in understanding the nature of interactions.
- Relating social interactions to content analysis: the content can give hint on the nature of the interaction and vice versa (e.g., users with more social interactions are more likely to have common interests).

To address the above issues, one needs to go beyond the static analysis approach, and develop dynamical models that will explicitly account for the interplay between the *content* of communication (topics) and the *structure* of communications (social networks). Such framework and corresponding algorithmic base will allow us to infer "polarizing" topics discussed in forums, identify evolving communities of interests, and examine the link between social and content dynamics.

To illustrate the advantages and the need for more fine–grained analysis, we now turn to a concrete example. Figure 1(a) provides a sample of discussion co-participation network from an online discussion forum. Each oval node represents a user and each square shows a discussion thread, while each arrow represents users participating in the thread. The numbers on the arrow represent the number of messages contributed to the thread. Ten discussion threads with 127 messages from 43 users are captured. Based on this network, we can identify users that have similar interests, cluster topics and/or users according to similarities, and so on. However, this network is too coarse–grained to get additional information about the social interactions. For instance, it does not say anything whether co–participating users have similar or conflicting views.

We now contrast the above network with a more fine–grained representation of forum dynamics. We performed a thorough manual analysis of threads, by taking into account the sequence of messages to construct response–to graph, and then manually annotating the *attitudes* of each message towards the one it was responding to. Figure 1(b) provides a signed attitude network from the same dataset as the one used for Figure 1(a). Each node represents a user and an arrow shows how one replies to the other.



*Proceedings of the NAACL HLT 2010 Workshop on Computational Linguistics in a World of Social Media*, pages 13–14,
Los Angeles, California, June 2010. ©2010 Association for Computational Linguistics

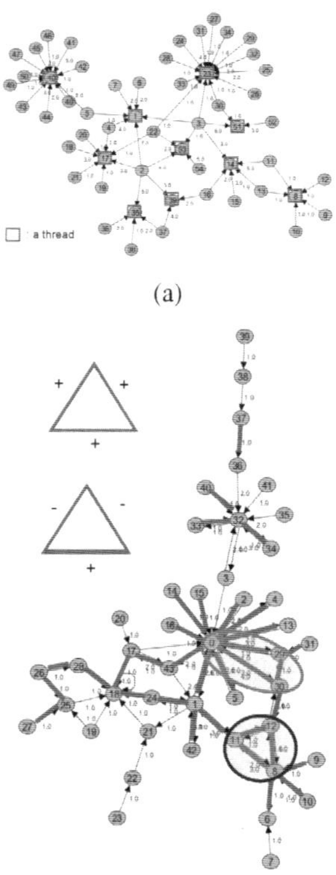


(a)

(b)

Figure 1: (a) Thread participation network; (b) Signed attitude network. In (b), the circles show two triangle relationships suggested by structural balance theory.

The numbers on the arrow represent the number of the reply–to occurrences, while the color of the link represents the attitude. Here we use a very loose definition of "attitude". Namely, positive (blue) attitude means that the posting user agrees with the previous comment or message, or expresses friendly sentiments. And negative attitude means disagreeing with the previous message or using outright offensive language. The resulting signed network differentiates links between the users (friends or foes).

Clearly, the resulting network is much more informative about the social interactions among the users. Remarkably, even for the small manually collected data-set, the resulting network reproduces some of the known features of signed networks from social sciences (Lescovec et. al., 2010; Wassermanc and Faust, 1994). For instance, the highlighted ovals show balanced triads: two friends with a common enemy and three mutual friends. This with structural balance theory, which suggests that in signed network particular triads with odd number of positive links (three mutual friends or two friends with a common enemy) are more plausible than other cases (e.g. three mutual foes). As we add more data, we expect more occurrences of such triads.

Our current research focuses on automating the above process of network construction and analysis. To this end, we have been developing approaches based on Dynamic Bayesian Networks where the nodes correspond to participating users and messages, and the edges encode probabilistic dependence between message content and user attitudes. In this framework, the content of a message depends on the previous message as well as on the attitude of the posting user towards both the content and the other user. The observables in this model are the messages (and in some cases, some user–attributes such as age, location etc). And the *unobservables* such as users' attitudes and social preferences are modeled through latent variables that need to be inferred. To be more specific, let $u_1$ and $u_2$ denote the variables describing the users, and $m_1, m_2, ...$ denote the message sequence. Within the proposed generative framework, the goal is to calculate the posterior probability $P(u_1, u_2|m_1, m_2, ...) \propto \pi(u_1)\pi(u_2)\pi(m_1|u_1)\prod_{t=2}^{K} P(m_t|m_{t-1}, u_{i=1,2})$. Here $\pi(.)$ are the priors, and $P(m_t|m_{t-1}, u_i)$ is a probability of seeing a particular response by the user $u_i$ to a message $m_{t-1}$, which will be estimated using annotated data and further refined through EM–type approach.

## References

Carvalho, V. and Cohen, W., On the collective classification of email speech acts. Proc. of SIGIR (2005).

Kang, J., Kim, J. and Shaw, E., Profiling Student Groups in Online Discussion with Network Analysis, Proc. of K-CAP wsp on Analyzing Social Media (2009).

Leskovec, J. Huttenlocher, D. Kleinberg. J. Signed Networks in Social Media. ACM SIGCHI Conference on Human Factors in Computing Systems (2010).

Park, S. Maurer F. A. Network Analysis of Stakeholders in Tool Visioning Process for Story Test Driven Development, Proc. IEEE Int'l Conf. on Engineering of Complex Computer Systems, (2009)

Ravi, S., Kim, J., Profiling Student Interactions in Threaded Discussions with Speech Act Classifiers. Proc. AI in Education (2007).

Wasserman, S. and Faust. K. Social Network Analysis: Methods and Applications. Camb. U. Press, (1994).

# Intelligent Linux Information Access by Data Mining: the ILIAD Project

**Timothy Baldwin,♠ David Martinez,♡ Richard B. Penman,♠ Su Nam Kim,♠**
**Marco Lui,♠ Li Wang♠** and **Andrew MacKinlay♠**
♠ Dept of Computer Science and Software Engineering, University of Melbourne, Australia
♡ NICTA Victoria Research Laboratory

**Abstract**

We propose an alternative to conventional information retrieval over Linux forum data, based on thread-, post- and user-level analysis, interfaced with an information retrieval engine via reranking.

## 1 Introduction

Due to the sheer scale of web data, simple keyword matching is an effective means of information access for many informational web queries. There still remain significant clusters of information access needs, however, where keyword matching is less successful. One such instance is technical web forums and mailing lists (collectively termed "forums" for the purposes of this paper): technical forums are a rich source of information when troubleshooting, and it is often possible to resolve technical queries/problems via web-archived data. The search facilities provided by forums and web search engines tend to be over-simplistic, however, and there is a desperate need for more sophisticated search (Xi et al., 2004; Seo et al., 2009), including: favouring threads which have led to a successful resolution; reflecting the degree of clarity/reproducibility of the proposed solution in a given thread; representing threads via their threaded rather than simple chronological structure; the ability to highlight key aspects of the thread, in terms of the problem description and solution which led to a successful resolution; and ideally, the ability to represent the problem and solution in normalised form via information extraction.

This paper provides a brief outline of an attempt to achieve these and other goals in the context of Linux web user forum data, in the form of the ILIAD (Intelligent Linux Information Access by Data Mining) project. Linux users and developers rely particularly heavily on web user forums and mailing lists, due to the nature of the community, which is highly decentralised — with massive proliferation of packages and distributions — and notoriously bad at maintaining up-to-date documentation at a level suitable for newbie and even intermediate users.

## 2 Project Outline

Our proposed solution is as follows: (1) crawl data from a variety of web user forums; (2) analyse each thread, to identify named entities and generate metadata; (3) analyse post-level linkages; (4) predict user-level features which are expected to impinge on the quality of search results; and finally (5) draw together the features from (1) to (4) to enhance the quality of a traditional ranked IR approach. We briefly review each step below. Given space limitations, we focus on outlining our interpretation of the task in this paper. For further details and results, the reader is referred to the key papers cited herein.

### 2.1 Crawling

The first step is to crawl data from a variety of forums and mailing lists, for which we have developed open-source scraping software in the form of SITESCRAPER.[1] SITESCRAPER is designed such that the user simply copies relevant content from a browser-rendered version of a given set of pages, which it interprets as a structured record, and translates into a generalised XPATH query.

### 2.2 Thread-level analysis

Next, we perform named entity recognition (NER) over each thread to identify entities such as package and distribution names, version numbers and snippets of code; as part of this, we perform version

[1] `http://sitescraper.googlecode.com/`



*Proceedings of the NAACL HLT 2010 Workshop on Computational Linguistics in a World of Social Media*, pages 15–16,
Los Angeles, California, June 2010. 

anchoring, in identifying what entity each version number relates to.

To generate thread-level metadata, we classify each thread for the following three features, based on an ordinal scale of 1–5 (Baldwin et al., 2007):

**Complete:** Is the problem description complete?

**Solved:** Is a solution provided in the thread?

**Task Oriented:** Is the thread about a specific problem?

We additionally automatically classify the nature of the thread content, in terms of, e.g., whether it contains documentation or installation details, or relates to software, hardware or programming.

Our experiments on thread-level classification are based on a set of 250 annotated threads from LinuxQuestions and other forums, as well as a dataset from CNET.

### 2.3 Post-level analysis

We automatically analyse the post-to-post discourse structure of each thread, in terms of which (preceding) post(s) each post relates to, and how, building off the work of Rosé et al. (1995) and Wolf and Gibson (2005). For example, a given post may refute the solution proposed in an earlier post, and also propose a novel solution in response to the initiating post.

Separately, we are developing techniques for identifying whether a new post to a given forum is sufficiently similar to other (ideally resolved) threads that the author should be prompted to first check the existing threads for redundancy before a new thread is initiated.

Our experiments on post-level analysis are, once again, based on data from LinuxQuestions and CNET.

### 2.4 User-level analysis

We are also experimenting with profiling users variously, based on a 5-point ordinal scale across a range of user characteristics. Our experiments are based on data from LinuxQuestions (Lui, 2009).

### 2.5 IR ranking

The various features are interfaced with an ad hoc information retrieval (IR) system via a learning-to-rank approach (Cao et al., 2007). In order to carry out IR evaluation, we have developed a set of queries and relevance judgements over a large-scale set of forum data.

Our experiments to date have been based on combination over three IR engines (LUCENE, ZETTAIR and LEMUR), and involved thread-level metadata only, but we have achieved encouraging results, suggesting that thread-level metadata can enhance IR effectiveness.

## 3 Conclusions

This paper provides an outline of the ILIAD project, focusing on the tasks of crawling, thread-level analysis, post-level analysis, user-level analysis and IR reranking. We have designed a series of class sets for the component tasks, and carried out experimentation over a range of data sources, achieving encouraging results.

### Acknowledgements

NICTA is funded by the Australian Government as represented by the Department of Broadband, Communications and the Digital Economy and the Australian Research Council through the ICT Centre of Excellence program.

## References

T Baldwin, D Martinez, and RB Penman. 2007. Automatic thread classification for Linux user forum information access. In *Proc of ADCS 2007*.

Z Cao, T Qin, TY Liu, MF Tsai, and H Li. 2007. Learning to rank: from pairwise approach to listwise approach. In *Proc of ICML 2007*.

M Lui. 2009. Impact of user characteristics on online forum classification tasks. Honours thesis, University of Melbourne. `http://repository.unimelb.edu.au/10187/5745`.

CP Rosé, B Di Eugenio, LS Levin, and C Van Ess-Dykema. 1995. Discourse processing of dialogues with multiple threads. In *Proc of ACL 1995*.

J Seo, WB Croft, and DA Smith. 2009. Online community search using thread structure. In *Proc of CIKM 2009*.

F Wolf and E Gibson. 2005. Representing discourse coherence: A corpus-based study. *Comp Ling*, 31(2).

W Xi, J Lind, and E Brill. 2004. Learning effective ranking functions for newsgroup search. In *Proc of SIGIR 2004*.

# Mining User Experiences from Online Forums: An Exploration*

**Valentin Jijkoun  Maarten de Rijke  Wouter Weerkamp**
ISLA, University of Amsterdam
Science Park 107
1098 XG Amsterdam, The Netherlands
jijkoun,m.derijke,w.weerkamp@uva.nl

**Paul Ackermans  Gijs Geleijnse**
Philips Research Europe
High Tech Campus 34
5656 AE Eindhoven, The Netherlands
paul.ackermans@philips.com
gijs.geleijnse@philips.com

## 1 Introduction

Recent years have shown a large increase in the usage of content creation platforms—blogs, community QA sites, forums, etc.—aimed at the general public.User generated data contains emotional, opinionated, sentimental, and personal posts. This characteristic makes it an interesting data source for exploring new types of linguistic analysis, as is demonstrated by research on, e.g., sentiment analysis [4], opinion retrieval [3], and mood detection [1].

We introduce the task of *experience mining*. Here, the goal is to gain insights into criteria that people formulate to judge or rate a product or its usage. These criteria can be formulated as the expectations that people have of the product in advance (i.e., the reasons to buy), but can also be expressed as reports of experiences while using the product and comparisons with other products. We focus on the latter: reports of experiences with products. In this paper, we define the task, describe guidelines for manual annotation and analyze linguistic features that can be used in an automatic experience mining system.

## 2 Motivation

Our main use-case is user-centered design for product development. User-centered design [2] is an innovation paradigm where users of a product are involved in each step of the research and development process. The first stage of the product design process is to identify unmet needs and demands of users for a specific product or a class of products. Forums, review sites, and mailing lists are platforms where people share experiences about a subject they care about. Although statements found in such platforms may not always be representative for the general user group, they can accelerate user-centered design.

Another use-case comes from online communities themselves. Users of online forums are often interested in other people's experiences with concrete products and/or solutions for specific problems. To quote one such user: *[t]he polls are the only information we have, though, except for individual [users] giving their own evaluations.* With the volume of online data increasing rapidly, users need improved access to previously reported experiences.

## 3 Experience mining

Experiences are particular instances of personally encountering or undergoing something. We want to identify experiences about a specific *target product*, that are *personal*, involve an *activity* related to the target and, moreover, are accompanied by *judgements or evaluative statements*. Experience mining is related to sentiment analysis and opinion retrieval, in that it involves identifying attitudes; the key difference is, however, that we are looking for *attitudes towards specific experiences* with products, not attitudes towards the products themselves.

## 4 An explorative study

To assess the feasibility of automatic experience mining, we carried out an explorative study: we asked human assessors to find experiences in actual forum data and then examined linguistic features likely to be useful for identifying experiences automatically.

*This research was supported by project STE-09-12 within the STEVIN programme funded by the Dutch and Flemish governments, and by the Netherlands Organisation for Scientific Research (NWO) under projects 640.001.501, 640.002.501, 612.066.512, 612.061.814, 612.061.815, 640.004.802.



*Proceedings of the NAACL HLT 2010 Workshop on Computational Linguistics in a World of Social Media*, pages 17–18,
Los Angeles, California, June 2010. 

| Feature | Mean and deviation in posts with exper. | without exper. |
|---|---|---|
| subjectivity score[2] | $0.07 \pm 0.23$ | $0.17 \pm 0.35$ |
| polarity score[2] | $0.87 \pm 0.30$ | $0.77 \pm 0.38$ |
| #words per post | $102.57 \pm 80.09$ | $52.46 \pm 53.24$ |
| #sentences per post | $6.00 \pm 4.16$ | $3.34 \pm 2.33$ |
| # words per sentence | $17.07 \pm 4.69$ | $15.71 \pm 7.61$ |
| #questions per post | $0.32 \pm 0.63$ | $0.54 \pm 0.89$ |
| $p$(post contains question) | $0.25 \pm 0.43$ | $0.33 \pm 0.47$ |
| #*I*'s per post | $5.76 \pm 4.75$ | $2.09 \pm 2.88$ |
| #*I*'s per sentence | $1.01 \pm 0.48$ | $0.54 \pm 0.60$ |
| $p$(sentence in post contains $I$) | $0.67 \pm 0.23$ | $0.40 \pm 0.35$ |
| #non-modal verbs per post | $19.62 \pm 15.08$ | $9.82 \pm 9.57$ |
| #non-modal verbs per sent. | $3.30 \pm 1.18$ | $2.82 \pm 1.37$ |
| #modal verbs per sent. | $0.22 \pm 0.22$ | $0.26 \pm 0.36$ |
| fraction of past-tense verbs | $0.26 \pm 0.17$ | $0.17 \pm 0.19$ |
| fraction of present tense verbs | $0.42 \pm 0.18$ | $0.41 \pm 0.23$ |

Table 1: Comparison of surface text features for posts with and without experience; $p(\cdot)$ denotes probability.

| With experience | Without experience |
|---|---|
| used 0.15, found 0.09, bought 0.07, tried 0.07, got 0.07, went 0.07, started 0.05, switched 0.04, liked 0.03, decided 0.03 | got 0.09, thought 0.09, switched 0.06, meant 0.06, used 0.06, went 0.06, ignored 0.03, quoted 0.03, discovered 0.03, heard 0.03 |

Table 2: Most frequent past tense verbs following *I* in posts with and without experience, with rel. frequencies.

We acquired data by crawling two forums on shaving,[1] with 111,268 posts written by 2,880 users.

**Manual assessments** Two assessors (both authors of this paper) were asked to search for posts on five specific target products using a standard keyword search, and label each result post as:

- reporting no experience, or
- reporting an off-target experience, or
- reporting an on-target experience.

Moreover, posts should be marked as reporting an experience only if (i) the author explicitly reports his or someone else's (a concrete person's) use of a product; and (ii) the author makes some conclusions/judgements about the experience.

In total, 203 posts were labeled by the two assessors, with 101 posts marked as reporting an experience by at least one assessor (71% of those an on-target experience). The inter-annotator agreement was 0.84, with Cohen's $\kappa = 0.71$. If we merge on- and off-target experience labels, the agreement is 0.88, with $\kappa = 0.76$. The high level of agreement demonstrates the validity of the task definition.

**Features for experience mining** We considered a number of linguistic features and compared posts reporting experience (on- or off-target) to the posts with no experience. Table 1 lists the features and the comparison results. Remarkably, the subjectivity score is lower for experience posts: this indicates that our task is indeed different from sentiment retrieval. Experience posts are on average twice as long as non-experience posts and contain more sentences with pronoun *I*. They also contain more content (non-modal) verbs, especially past tense verbs. Table 2 presents a more detailed analysis of the verb use. Experience posts appear to contain more verbs referring to concrete actions rather than to attitude and perception. It is still to be seen, though, whether this informal observation can be quantified using resources such as standard semantic verb classification (*state, process, action*), WordNet verb hierarchy or FrameNet semantic frames.

[1]www.shavemyface.com, www.menessentials.com/community

[2]Computed using LingPipe: http://alias-i.com/lingpipe

## 5 Conclusions

We introduced the novel task of experience mining. Users of products share their experiences, and mining these could help define requirements for next-generation products. We developed annotation guidelines for labeling experiences, and used them to annotate data from online forums. An initial exploration revealed multiple features that might prove useful for automatic labeling via classification.

## References

[1] K. Balog, G. Mishne, and M. de Rijke. Why are they excited?: identifying and explaining spikes in blog mood levels. In *EACL '06*, pages 207–210, 2006.

[2] B. Buxton. *Sketching User Experiences: Getting the Design Right and the Right Design.* Morgan Kaufmann Publishers Inc., 2007.

[3] I. Ounis, C. Macdonald, M. de Rijke, G. Mishne, and I. Soboroff. Overview of the TREC 2006 Blog Track. In *TREC 2006*, 2007.

[4] B. Pang and L. Lee. Opinion mining and sentiment analysis. *Found. Trends Inf. Retr.*, 2(1-2):1–135, 2008.

# Social Links from Latent Topics in Microblogs*

**Kriti Puniyani and Jacob Eisenstein and Shay Cohen and Eric P. Xing**
School of Computer Science
Carnegie Mellon University
{kpuniyan,jacobeis,scohen,epxing}@cs.cmu.edu

## 1 Introduction

Language use is overlaid on a network of social connections, which exerts an influence on both the topics of discussion and the ways that these topics can be expressed (Halliday, 1978). In the past, efforts to understand this relationship were stymied by a lack of data, but social media offers exciting new opportunities. By combining large linguistic corpora with explicit representations of social network structures, social media provides a new window into the interaction between language and society. Our long term goal is to develop joint sociolinguistic models that explain the social basis of linguistic variation.

In this paper we focus on *microblogs*: internet journals in which each entry is constrained to a few words in length. While this platform receives high-profile attention when used in connection with major news events such as natural disasters or political turmoil, less is known about the themes that characterize microblogging on a day-to-day basis. We perform an exploratory analysis of the content of a well-known microblogging platform (Twitter), using topic models to uncover latent semantic themes (Blei et al., 2003). We then show that these latent topics are predictive of the network structure; without any supervision, they predict which other microblogs a user is likely to follow, and to whom microbloggers will address messages. Indeed, our topical link predictor outperforms a competitive supervised alternative from traditional social network analysis. Finally, we explore the application of supervision to our topical link predictor, using regression to learn weights that emphasize topics of particular relevance to the social network structure.

## 2 Data

We acquired data from Twitter's streaming "Gardenhose" API, which returned roughly 15% of all messages sent over a period of two weeks in January 2010. This comprised 15GB of compressed data; we aimed to extract a representative subset by first sampling 500 people who posted at least sixteen messages over this period, and then "crawled" at most 500 randomly-selected followers of each of these original authors. The resulting data includes 21,306 users, 837,879 messages, and 10,578,934 word tokens.

**Text** Twitter contains highly non-standard orthography that poses challenges for early-stage text processing.[1] We took a conservative approach to tokenization, splitting only on whitespaces and apostrophes, and eliminating only token-initial and token-final punctuation characters. Two markers are used to indicate special tokens: `#`, indicating a topic (e.g. `#curling`); and `@`, indicating that the message is addressed to another user. Topic tokens were included after stripping the leading `#`, but address tokens were removed. All terms occurring less than 50 times were removed, yielding a vocabulary of 11,425 terms. Out-of-vocabulary items were classified as either words, URLs, or numbers. To ensure a fair evaluation, we removed "retweets" – when a user reposts verbatim the message of another user – if the original message author is also part of the dataset.

**Links** We experiment with two social graphs extracted from the data: a **follower graph** and a **communication graph**. The follower graph places directed edges between users who have chosen to follow each other's updates; the message graph places a directed edge between users who have addressed messages to each other (using the `@` symbol). Huberman et al. (2009) argue that the communication graph captures direct interactions and is thus a more accurate representation of the true underlying social structure, while the follower graph contains more connections than could possibly be maintained in a realistic social network.

*We thank the reviews for their helpful suggestions and Brendan O'Connor for making the Twitter data available.

[1]For example, some tweets use punctuation for tokenization (`You look like a retired pornstar!lmao`) while others use punctuation inside the token (`l0v!n d!s th!ng call3d l!f3`).



*Proceedings of the NAACL HLT 2010 Workshop on Computational Linguistics in a World of Social Media*, pages 19–20,
Los Angeles, California, June 2010. 

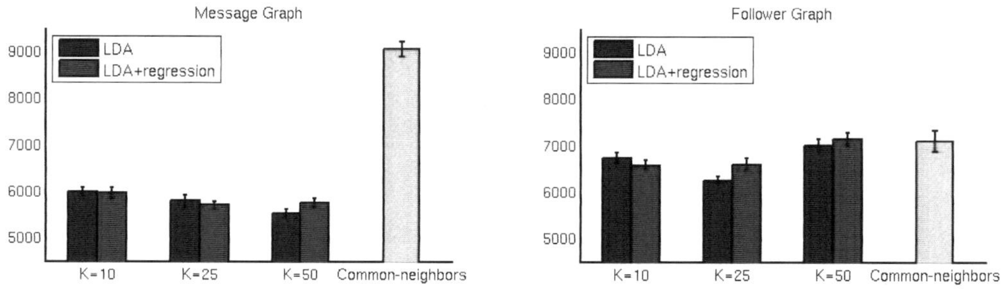


Figure 1: Mean rank of test links (lower is better), reported over 4-fold cross-validation. Common-neighbors is a network-based method that ignores text; the LDA (Latent Dirichlet Allocation) methods are grouped by number of latent topics.

## 3 Method

We constructed a topic model over twitter messages, identifying the latent themes that characterize the corpus. In standard topic modeling methodology, topics define distributions over vocabulary items, and each document contains a set of latent topic proportions (Blei et al., 2003). However, the average message on Twitter is only sixteen word tokens, which is too sparse for traditional topic modeling; instead, we gathered together all of the messages from a given user into a single document. Thus our model learns the latent topics that characterize *authors*, rather than messages.

Authors with similar topic proportions are likely to share interests or dialect, suggesting potential social connections. Author similarity can be quantified without supervision by taking the dot product of the topic proportions. If labeled data is available (a partially observed network), then regression can be applied to learn weights for each topic. Chang and Blei (2009) describe such a regression-based predictor, which takes the form $\exp\left(-\eta^T(\bar{z}_i - \bar{z}_j) \circ (\bar{z}_i - \bar{z}_j) - \nu\right)$, denoting the predicted strength of connection between authors $i$ and $j$. Here $\bar{z}_i$ ($\bar{z}_j$) refers to the expected topic proportions for user $i$ ($j$), $\eta$ is a vector of learned regression weights, and $\nu$ is an intercept term which is only necessary if a the link prediction function must return a probability. We used the updates from Chang and Blei to learn $\eta$ in a post hoc fashion, after training the topic model.

## 4 Results

We constructed topic models using an implementation of variational inference[2] for Latent Dirichlet Allocation (LDA). The results of the run with the best variational bound on 50 topics can be found at `http://sailing.cs.cmu.edu/socialmedia/naacl10ws/`. While many of the topics focus on content (for example, electronics and sports), others capture distinct languages and even dialect variation. Such dialects are particularly evident in stopwords (`you` versus `u`). Structured topic models that explicitly handle these two orthogonal axes of linguistic variation are an intriguing possibility for future work.

We evaluate our topic-based approach for link prediction on both the **message** and **follower** graphs, comparing against an approach that only considers the network structure. Liben-Nowell and Kleinberg (2003) perform a quantitative comparison of such approaches, finding that the relatively simple technique of counting the number of shared neighbors between two nodes is a surprisingly competitive predictor of whether they are linked; we call this approach common-neighbors. We evaluate this method and our own supervised LDA+regression approach by hiding half of the edges in the graph, and predicting them from the other half.

For each author in the dataset, we apply each method to rank all possible links; the evaluation computes the average rank of the true links that were held out (for our data, a random baseline would score $10653$ – half the number of authors in the network). As shown in Figure 1, topic-based link prediction outperforms the alternative that considers only the graph structure. Interestingly, post hoc regression on the topic proportions did not consistently improve performance, though joint learning may do better (e.g., Chang and Blei, 2009). The text-based approach is especially strong on the message graph, while the link-based approach is more competitive on the followers graph; a model that captures both features seems a useful direction for future work.

[2] `http://www.cs.princeton.edu/~blei/lda-c`

## References

D. Blei, A. Ng, and M. Jordan. 2003. Latent Dirichlet allocation. *Journal of Machine Learning Research*, 3:993–1022.

J. Chang and D. Blei. 2009. Hierarchical relational models for document networks. *Annals of Applied Statistics*.

M.A.K. Halliday. 1978. *Language as social semiotic: The social interpretation of language and meaning*. University Park Press.

Bernardo Huberman, Daniel M. Romero, and Fang Wu. 2009. Social networks that matter: Twitter under the microscope. *First Monday*, 14(1–5), January.

D. Liben-Nowell and J. Kleinberg. 2003. The link prediction problem for social networks. In *Proc. of CIKM*.

# Automatic Detection of Tags for Political Blogs

**Khairun-nisa Hassanali**
Human Language Technology Institute
The University of Texas at Dallas
Richardson, TX 75080, USA
nisa@hlt.utdallas.edu

**Vasileios Hatzivassiloglou**
Human Language Technology Institute
The University of Texas at Dallas
Richardson, TX 75080, USA
vh@hlt.utdallas.edu

## Abstract

This paper describes a technique for automatically tagging political blog posts using SVM's and named entity recognition. We compare the quality of the tags detected by this approach to earlier approaches in other domains, observing effects from the political domain and benefits from NLP techniques complementary to the core SVM method.

## 1 Introduction

Political blogs are a particular type of communication platform that combines analyses provided by the blog owner or a team of regular contributors with shorter, but far more numerous, entries by visitors. Given the enthusiasm that activities for or against a particular politician or party can generate, political blogs are a vibrant part of the blogosphere: more than 38,500 blogs specifically dedicated to politics exist in the US alone according to Technorati, and some of the more active ones attract more than 30 million unique visitors each month (double that number just before major elections).

Political blogs provide a wealth of factual information about political events and activities, but also by their nature are colored by strong opinions. They are therefore a particularly attractive target for semantic analysis methods using natural language processing technology. In fact, the past two years have brought an increased number of collaborations between NLP researchers and political scientists using data from political sources, including two special issues of leading political science journals on such topics (see (Cardie and Wilkerson, 2008) for an overview). Our motivation for working with this kind of data is the construction of a system that collates information across blog posts, combines evidence to numerically rate attitudes of blogs on different topics, and traces the evolution of these attitudes across time and in response to events. To enable these tasks, we first identify the major topics that each blog post covers. In the present paper, we describe our recognizer of blog post topics. We show that, perhaps because of the richness of political blogs in named entities, an SVM-based keyword learning approach can be complemented with named entity recognition and co-reference detection to achieve precision and recall scores higher than those reported by earlier topic recognition systems in other domains.

## 2 Related Work

In our approach, as in earlier published work, we take *tags* assigned by many blogs to individual blog posts as a reference list of the topics covered by that post. Tags are single words or short phrases, most often noun phrases, and are usually chosen by each post's authors without a controlled vocabulary; examples include "Michigan", "George Bush", "democracy", and "health care". Earlier work in predicting tags includes (Mishne, 2006), who adopts a collaborative filtering approach; in contrast, we rely on training classifiers from earlier posts in each blog. Our approach is more similar to (Sood et al., 2007) and (Wang and Davison, 2008) who use different machine learning techniques applied to a training set. We differ from the last two approaches in our addition of proper noun and named entity recognition methods to our core SVM classifiers, in our exploration of specifically political data, and in our subsequent use of



*Proceedings of the NAACL HLT 2010 Workshop on Computational Linguistics in a World of Social Media*, pages 21–22,
Los Angeles, California, June 2010. 

the predicted tags (for semantic analysis rather than tag set compression or query expansion).

## 3 Data

We collected data from two major political blogs, Daily Kos (`www.dailykos.com`) and Red State (`www.redstate.com`). Red State is a conservative political blog whereas Daily Kos is a liberal political blog. Both these blogs are widely read and tag each of their blog entries. We collected data from both these blogs over a period of two years (January 2008 – February 2010). We collected a total of 100,000 blog posts from Daily Kos and 70,000 blog posts from Red State and a total of 787,780 tags across both blogs (an average of 4.63 tags per post).

## 4 Methods

We used SVM Light (Joachims, 2002) to predict the tags for a given blog post. We constructed one classifier for each of the tags present in the training set. The features used were counts of each word encountered in the title or the body of a post (two counts per word), further subdivided by whether the word appears in any tags in the training data or not, and whether it is a synonym of known tag words. We extract the top five proposed tags for each post, corresponding to the five highest scoring SVM classifiers.

We also attempt to detect the main entities being talked about. We perform shallow parsing and extract noun phrases and then proper nouns. The most frequent proper NPs are probable tags. We also added named entity recognition and co-reference resolution using the OpenNLP toolkit (`maxent.sourceforge.net`). We found that named entity recognition proposes additional useful tags while the effect of co-reference resolution is marginal, mostly because of limited success in actually matching co-referent entities.

## 5 Results and Evaluation

For evaluating our methods, we used 2,681 posts from Daily Kos and 571 posts from Red State. We compared the tags assigned by our tagger to the original tags of the blog post, using an automated method (Figure 1). A tag was considered a match if it exactly matched the original tag or was a word super set – for example "health care system" is considered a match to "health care". We also manually evaluated the relevance of the proposed tags on a small portion of our test set (100 posts).

| Method | Precision | Recall | F-Score |
|---|---|---|---|
| Single word SVM | 27.3% | 60.3% | 37.6% |
| + Stemming | 26.1% | 59.5% | 36.3% |
| + Proper Nouns | 36.5% | 56.8% | 44.4% |
| Named Entities | 48.4% | 49.1% | 48.7% |
| All Combined | 21.1% | 65.0% | 31.9% |
| Manual Scoring | **67.0%** | **75.0%** | **70.8%** |
| Single word SVM | 19.0% | 30.0% | 23.3% |
| + Stemming | 22.0% | 30.2% | 25.5% |
| + Proper Nouns | 46.3% | 54.0% | 49.9% |
| Named Entities | **60.1%** | 41.5% | 49.1% |
| All Combined | 20.3% | **65.7%** | 31.0% |
| Manual Scoring | 47.0% | 62.0% | **53.5%** |

Figure 1: Results on Daily Kos (top) and Red State (bottom) data. Best scores in bold.

## 6 Conclusion

We described and evaluated a tool for automatically tagging political blog posts. Political blogs differ from other blogs as they often involve named entities (politicians, organizations, and places). Therefore, tagging of political blog posts benefits from using basic name entity recognition to improve the tagging. The recall in particular exceeds the score obtained by earlier techniques applied to other domains (Sood et al. (2007) report precision of 13% and recall of 23%; Wang and Davison (2008) report precision of 45% and recall of 23%).

## References


Claire Cardie and John Wilkerson (editors). "Special Volume: Text Annotation for Political Science Research". *Journal of Information Technology and Politics*, 5(1):1-6, 2008.

Thorsten Joachims. SVM-Light. 2002. http://www.svmlight.joachims.org.

Gilad Mishne. "AutoTag: A Collaborative Approach to Automated Tag Assignment for Weblog Posts". In *Proceedings of WWW*, 2006.

Sanjay C. Sood, Sara H. Owsley, Kristian J. Hammond, and Larry Birnbaum. "TagAssist: Automatic Tag Suggestion for Blog Posts". In *Proceedings of ICWSM*, 2007.

Jian Wang and Brian D. Davison. "Explorations in Tag Suggestion and Query Expansion". In *Proceedings of SSM '08*, 2008.

# Twitter in Mass Emergency: What NLP Techniques Can Contribute

**William J. Corvey[1], Sarah Vieweg[2], Travis Rood[1] & Martha Palmer[1]**
[1]Department of Linguistics, [2]ATLAS Institute
University of Colorado
Boulder, CO 80309
William.Corvey, Sarah.Vieweg, Travis.Rood, Martha.Palmer@colorado.edu

## Abstract

We detail methods for entity span identification and entity class annotation of Twitter communications that take place during times of mass emergency. We present our motivation, method and preliminary results.

## 1 Introduction

During times of mass emergency, many turn to Twitter to gather and disperse relevant, timely information (Starbird et al. 2010; Vieweg et al. 2010). However, the sheer amount of information now communicated via Twitter during these time- and safety-critical situations can make it difficult for individuals to locate personally meaningful and actionable information. In this paper, we discuss natural language processing (NLP) techniques designed for Twitter data that will lead to the location and extraction of specific information during times of mass emergency.

## 2 Twitter Use in Mass Emergency

Twitter communications are comprised of 140-character messages called "tweets." During times of mass emergency, Twitter users send detailed information that may help those affected to better make critical decisions.

Our goal is to develop techniques to automatically identify crucial pieces of information in these tweets. This process will lead to the automatic extraction of information that helps people understand the situation "on the ground" during mass emergencies. Relevant information would include such things as warnings, road closures, and evacuations among other timely information.

## 3 The Annotation Process

A foundational level of linguistic annotation for many natural language processing tasks is Named Entity (or nominal entity) tagging (Bikel 1999). Typical labeled entities that were included in the Automatic Content Extraction (ACE) guidelines (LDC 2004) are: Person, Location, Organization, and Facility, the four maximal entity classes. Our preliminary annotation task consists of identifying the syntactic span and entity class for these four types of entities in a pilot set of Twitter data (200 tweets from a data set generated during the 2009 Oklahoma grassfires). In future annotation, the ontology will be expanded to include event and relation annotations, as well as additional subclasses of the entities now examined. Annotations are done using Knowtator (Ogren 2006), a tool built within the Protégé framework (http://protege.stanford.edu/). The ontology development is data-driven; as such it is likely that certain ACE annotations will never emerge and other annotations (such as disaster-relevant materials) will be necessary additions.

Three annotators undertook pilot annotation as part of the construction of preliminary annotation guidelines; the top pairwise ITA score is reported below. Twitter data makes reference to numerous entity spans that are of specific interest to this annotation task, such as road intersections and multi-word named entities. The example below, from the pilot annotation set, shows a relatively simple span delineation.

[$_{\text{PERSON}}$ Velma area residents]: [$_{\text{PERSON}}$ Officials] say to take [$_{\text{FACILTY}}$ Old Hwy 7] to [$_{\text{FACILTY}}$ Speedy G] to safely evacuate. [$_{\text{LOCATION}}$ Stephens Co Fairgrounds] in [$_{\text{LOCATION}}$ Duncan] for shelter



*Proceedings of the NAACL HLT 2010 Workshop on Computational Linguistics in a World of Social Media*, pages 23–24,
Los Angeles, California, June 2010. 

Because of the varying length of entities, annotators cannot be given simple rules for deciding the spans for annotations. This difficulty is reflected in markedly lower rates for span identification inter-annotator agreement (IAA) rates than for simple class assignment.

## 4 Preliminary Results

IAA calculations were performed using the Knowtator IAA functionality. When annotations are required to be both the same span and class, the pilot annotation yielded an F-score of 56.27 (An additional 4% have exact span matches but different classes). However, when annotations are required to have the same class assignment but only overlapping spans, this F-score rises to 72.85. While Facility and Location are the most commonly confused classes, span-matching remains a difficult issue for all entity classes.

## 5 Discussion

While these ITA rates are significantly lower than published results from previous ACE annotation efforts (LDC 2004), we believe that the crisis communications domain, particularly with regard to Twitter analysis, provides challenges not encountered in newswire, broadcast transcripts, or newspaper data. First, determining the maximal span of interest for a given class assignment is non-trivial. The constraint of 140 characters necessarily results in very limited syntactic and semantic contexts, making spans and entity class assignments much harder to determine.

A large source of disagreement was on the treatment of coordinated or listed noun phrases. In certain contexts, each entity (*cities* below) requires its own span (e.g. "Firestorms in Oklahoma. [*Midwest City*], [*Lake Draper*]. Some houses lost"), whereas in other contexts we find *multiple* entities per span (e.g. "Midwest City to evacuate between SE 15th and Rena and Anderson and Hiwassee also [*Turtlewood, Wingsong, and Oakwood additions*]"). Equally, class assignment cannot be a mechanistic process or accomplished by reference to lists, as it is important to distinguish between cases where terms have been elided due to limited space and cases where no elision has taken place. For instance, the entity "Attorney General" (as opposed to "Attorney General's Office") might be annotated 'Person' or 'Organization' depending on context, or simply ambiguous, i.e. lacking sufficient context. It is primarily these unclear cases of class assignment that will require careful discussion in the annotation guidelines and in future mappings to an ontology.

In summary, this pilot study represents a new application of ACE annotation practices to a uniquely challenging domain. We outline issues that place special demands on annotators and future directions for ongoing research. We are confident that as we refine our guidelines and provide more cues and examples for the annotators that the determination of spans and entity classes will improve.

## Acknowledgments

This work is supported by the US National Science Foundation IIS-0546315 and IIS-0910586 but does not represent the views of the NSF. This work was conducted using the Protégé resource, supported by grant LM007885 from the US NLM.

## References

Daniel M. Bikel, Richard Schwartz and Ralph M. Weischedel. 1999. *An Algorithm that Learns What's in a Name*. In: the Machine Learning Journal Special Issue on Natural Language Learning.

George Doddington, A. Mitchell, M. Przybocki, L. Ramshaw, S. Strassel, and R. Weischedel. (2004). *The Automatic Content Extraction (ACE) Program – Tasks, Data, and Evaluation.* In: Proceedings of Conference on Language Resources and Evaluation (LREC 2004).

Kate Starbird, Leysia Palen, Amanda L. Hughes and Sarah Vieweg. 2010. *Chatter on The Red: What Hazards Threat Reveals About the Social Life of Microblogged Information.* In: Proc. CSCW 2010. ACM Press.

LDC, 2004, Automatic Content Extraction [www.ldc.upenn.edu/Projects/ACE/]

Philip Ogren. 2006. *Knowtator: A Protégé plug-in for annotated corpus construction*. In : Proceedings of the 2006 Conference of the North American Chapter of the Association for Computational Linguistics on Human Language Technology 2006. ACM Press.

Sarah Vieweg, Amanda L. Hughes, Kate Starbird and Leysia Palen. 2010. *Microblogging During Two Natural Hazards Events: What Twitter May Contribute to Situational Awareness.* In: Proc. CHI 2010. ACM Press.

# The Edinburgh Twitter Corpus

**Saša Petrović**
School of Informatics
University of Edinburgh
`sasa.petrovic@ed.ac.uk`

**Miles Osborne**
School of Informatics
University of Edinburgh
`miles@inf.ed.ac.uk`

**Victor Lavrenko**
School of Informatics
University of Edinburgh
`vlavrenk@inf.ed.ac.uk`

## Abstract

We describe the first release of our corpus of 97 million Twitter posts. We believe that this data will prove valuable to researchers working in social media, natural language processing, large-scale data processing, and similar areas.

## 1 Introduction

In the recent years, the microblogging service Twitter has become a popular tool for expressing opinions, broadcasting news, and simply communicating with friends. People often comment on events in real time, with several hundred micro-blogs (*tweets*) posted each second for significant events. Despite this popularity, there still does not exist a publicly available corpus of Twitter posts. In this paper we describe the first such corpus collected over a period of two months using the Twitter streaming API.[1] Our corpus contains 97 million tweets, and takes up 14 GB of disk space uncompressed. The corpus is distributed under a Creative Commons Attribution-NonCommercial-ShareAlike license[2] and can be obtained at `http://demeter.inf.ed.ac.uk/`. Each tweet has the following information:

- timestamp – time (in GMT) when the tweet was written
- anonymized username – the author of the tweet, where the author's original Twitter username is replaced with an id of type *userABC*. We anonymize the usernames in this way to avoid malicious use of the data (e.g., by spammers). Note that usernames are anonymized consistently, i.e., every time user $A$ is mentioned in the stream, he is replaced with the same id.
- posting method – method used to publish the tweet (e.g., web, API, some Twitter client). Given that there are dozen of Twitter clients in use today, we believe this information could be very useful in determining, e.g., any differences in content that comes through different clients.

The format of our data is very simple. Each line has the following format:

timestamp \t username \t tweet \t client

where \t is the tab character, and client is the program used for posting the tweet. Note that the additional whitespaces seen above are only added for readability, and don't exist in the corpus.

Table 1: N-gram statistics.

| N-grams | tokens | unique |
|---|---|---|
| Unigrams | 2,263,886,631 | 31,883,775 |
| Bigrams | 2,167,567,986 | 174,785,693 |
| Trigrams | 2,072,595,131 | 948,850,470 |
| 4-grams | 1,980,386,036 | 1,095,417,876 |

## 2 Corpus statistics

We collected the corpus from a period spanning November 11th 2009 until February 1st 2010. As was already mentioned, the data was collected through Twitter's streaming API and is thus a representative sample of the entire stream. Table 1 shows the basic n-gram statistics – note that our corpus contains over 2 billion words. We made no attempt to distinguish between English and non-English tweets, as we believe that a multilingual stream might be of use for various machine translation experiments.

Table 2 shows some basic statistics specific to the Twitter stream. In particular, we give the number of users that posted the tweets, the number of links (URLs) in the corpus, the number of topics and the number of replies. From the first two rows of Table 2

[1] `http://stream.twitter.com/`

[2] `http://creativecommons.org/licenses/by-nc-sa/3.0/legalcode`



*Proceedings of the NAACL HLT 2010 Workshop on Computational Linguistics in a World of Social Media*, pages 25–26,
Los Angeles, California, June 2010. 

Table 2: Twitter-specific statistics.

| | Unique | Total |
|---|---|---|
| tweets | - | 96,369,326 |
| users | 9,140,015 | - |
| links | - | 20,627,320 |
| topics | 1,416,967 | 12,588,431 |
| replies | 5,426,030 | 54,900,387 |
| clients | 33,860 | - |

Table 3: Most cited Twitter users

| Username | number of replies |
|---|---|
| @justinbieber | 279,622 |
| @nickjonas | 95,545 |
| @addthis | 56,761 |
| @revrunwisdom | 51,203 |
| @ | 50,565 |
| @luansantanaevc | 49,106 |
| @donniewahlberg | 46,126 |
| @eduardosurita | 36,495 |
| @fiuk | 33,570 |
| @ddlovato | 32,327 |

Table 4: Most popular topics on Twitter

| Topic | number of occurences |
|---|---|
| #nowplaying | 255,715 |
| #ff | 220,607 |
| #jobs | 181,205 |
| #fb | 144,835 |
| #39;s | 110,150 |
| #formspringme | 85,775 |
| #tcot | 77,294 |
| #fail | 56,730 |
| #tinychat | 56,174 |
| #mm | 52,971 |

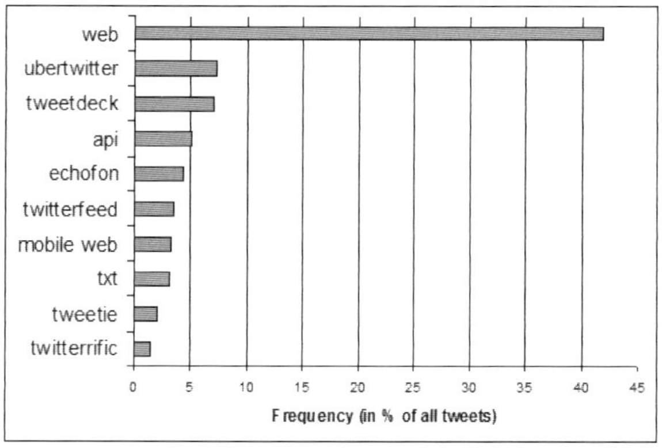


Figure 1: Different sources of tweets.

we can see that the average number of tweets per user is 10.5. Topics are defined as single word preceded by a # symbol, and replies are single words preceded by a @ symbol. This is the standard way Twitter users add metadata to their posts. For topics and replies, we give both the number of unique tokens and the total number of tokens.

Table 3 shows a list of 10 users which received the most replies. The more replies a user receives, more influential we might consider him. We can see that the two top ranking users are Justin Bieber and Nick Jonas, two teenage pop-stars who apparently have a big fan base on Twitter. In fact, six out of ten users on the list are singers, suggesting that many artists have turned to Twitter as a means of communicating with their fans. Note also that one of the entries is an empty username – this is probably a consequence of mistakes people make when posting a reply.

Similarly to Table 3, Table 4 shows the ten most popular topics in our corpus. We can see that the most popular topics include music (#nowplaying, #mm – music monday), jobs ads, facebook updates (#fb), politics (#tcot – top conservatives on Twitter), and random chatter (#ff – follow friday, #tinychat, #fail, #formspringme). The topic #39;s is an error in interpreting the apostrophe sign, which has the ascii value 39 (decimal).

Figure 1 shows the ten most popular clients used for posting to Twitter. Despite the large amount of different Twitter clients used (over 33 thousand, cf. Table 2), figure 1 shows that almost 80% of all the tweets in our corpus were posted using one of the top ten most popular clients. We can see that traditional posting through the Twitter web site is still by far the most popular method, while UberTwitter and TweetDeck seem to be the next most popular choices.

## 3 Conclusion

In this paper we presented a corpus of almost 100 million tweets which we made available for public use. Basic properties of the corpus are given and a simple analysis of the most popular users and topics revealed that Twitter is in large part used to talk about music by communicating both with artists and other fans. We believe that this corpus could be a very useful resource for researchers dealing with social media, natural language processing, or large-scale data processing.

# Labelling and Spatio-Temporal Grounding of News Events

**Bea Alex**
School of Informatics
University of Edinburgh, UK
balex@staffmail.ed.ac.uk

**Claire Grover**
School of Informatics
University of Edinburgh, UK
grover@inf.ed.ac.uk

## Abstract

This paper describes work in progress on labelling and spatio-temporal grounding of news events as part of a news analysis system that is under development.

## 1 Introduction: News Event Analysis

The SYNC3 project[1] is developing a system that tracks news events and related blogs. A news event is defined like a TDT event as something that happened at a particular time and place (TDT, 2004). It constitutes a cluster of news items which all report on the same event. The system crawls news sources and clusters incoming news items. These clusters are then processed by a labelling and a relation extraction component. The former determines document and event-level labels and the later derives temporal, geographic and causal relations between events. Related blog posts are connected to news events and analysed for sentiment. In the user interface, users can search and select news events and related blogs, add comments and interact with other users. Users will also be able to visualise related news events in a map interface and timeline. In this paper, the focus is on the labelling of news events.

The input into the news event labeller is made up of news event clusters containing one or more news items from different sources. Each news item is fed through a linguistic processing pipeline, including named entity recognition, date and geo-resolution. Each cluster is then labelled with a LABEL (a title summarising the news event), a DESCRIPTION (the first sentence of a document), a LOCATION (the location where the event took place) and a DATE (the date of the event). We first compute this information for every news item as a document summary and then select the most representative document summary of the news event cluster.

[1] http://www.sync3.eu

### 1.1 News Event Label

News titles tend to be appropriate summaries of news items and events. They are coherent phrases or sentences that are understood by users. We therefore implemented variations of title labelling (Manning et al., 2008) made up of document-level title detection and cluster-level title selection. The first step is done by iterating through the sentences of a document and settling on a title if certain criteria are met (e.g. number of tokens is 3 or more, sentence does not match a set of filter strings etc.). Given all document titles, we select as the most representative LABEL:

1. the LABEL of the first published news item,
2. the LABEL of the news item closest to the cluster centroid or
3. the LABEL with the largest ratio of terms common to all titles divided by title length

The 1st method assumes that a news item which first reports an event is breaking news and most interesting to users. News items following it will provide the same or further information. The 2nd method assumes that the news item most representative of the cluster statistically summarises the news event best. The last method assumes that the most succinct title with the most common vocabulary in all titles is most informative about a news event.

### 1.2 News Event Location

We use the Edinburgh Geoparser (Tobin et al., 2010) to recognise location names and ground them to the GeoNames gazetteer.[2] Besides latitudes, longitudes and GeoNames IDs, we also assign population size and type of location (e.g. populated place, country etc.). Our Geoparser yields 81.2% accuracy when evaluating on SpatialML (Mani et al., 2008). It also compares favourably with Yahoo! Placemaker[3] in an end-to-end run.

[2] http://www.geonames.org

[3] http://developer.yahoo.com/geo/placemaker



*Proceedings of the NAACL HLT 2010 Workshop on Computational Linguistics in a World of Social Media*, pages 27–28,
Los Angeles, California, June 2010. 

We only consider locations grounded to lat/long values as potential news item locations, therefore restricting the set to more accurately recognised ones. We select the first location in the LABEL and DESCRIPTION or (if none can be found) either the first or most frequent location in the news item. The news item location associated with the most representative cluster LABEL is selected as the news event location. To allow consistency of the information, we treat all caps locations in the DESCRIPTION of each article as reporter locations and will investigate the percentage of cases in which this location is the same as, near or different from the news event location. We will also experiment with limiting the search space of locations to the excerpts of a news item that are evidence for it being part of its cluster.

### 1.3 News Event Date

We choose the publication date of the earliest published news item in the cluster as the news event date. Our linguistic processing recognises absolute, relative and under-specified temporal expressions (MUC-style TIMEX elements), normalises them and grounds them to a single number representation (the 1st of January 1 AD being 0). This enables us to determine the day of the week, resolve relative dates and compute temporal precedence on a timeline. We are working towards evaluating the performance of the temporal expression recognition on the Timebank corpus (Pustejovsky et al., 2003).

## 2 Clustered News Data

We are developing our components using a static set of clusters containing 12,547 documents from 9 different news sources (AP: 16.7%, BBC: 12.9%, CNN: 5.2%, NYT: 9.2%, Reuters: 11.1%, Ria Novosti: 4.9%, USA TODAY: 12.3%, WP: 6.6% and Xinhua: 20.7%) which were crawled between May 20th and June 3rd 2009. The clustering of these documents changes in regular intervals. The current release contains 7,456 clusters with an average of 1.7 news items per cluster with up to 41 news items. 2,259 clusters (30.3%) contain 2 or more news items of which 1,091 (48.3%) contain news items from at least 2 sources. The duration of a news event is 4 days or less (<=1 day: 85.3%, 2 days: 12.4%, 3 days: 2.0%, 4 days: 0.3%).

The Geoparser extracts 188,932 locations assigned with lat/longs from this data. Using the 3rd labelling method, we currently detect a news event location in 7,325 of 7,456 news events (98.3%). If we only consider locations in news item LABELs and DESCRIPTIONs this figure drops to 83%. 117 clusters contain no location. An error analysis will show if this is due to false negatives or inexplicit locations.

## 3 Summary and Future Work

We have presented ongoing work on news event labelling, with a focus on title labelling and spatio-temporal grounding of news events, and have presented some initial statistics on development data.

We are in the process of creating gold standard data with which we can test the performance of the news event labelling. This will allow us to determine the appropriateness of the news event labels as well as the accuracy of news event locations and dates and enable us to fine-tune the labelling process. Our future work also includes identifying geographical, temporal and causal relations between news events for story detection.

Both the clustering of news into news events and their analysis are crucial for structuring and analysing the blogosphere accordingly, as one aim of SYNC3 is to extract news-event-related blog posts and identify their sentiment.

## Acknowledgements

We would like to thank all project partners of the SYNC3 project (FP7-231854).

## References

I. Mani, J. Hitzeman, J. Richer, D. Harris, R. Quimby, and B. Wellner. 2008. SpatialML: Annotation scheme, corpora, and tools. In *Proceedings of LREC'08.*

C. D. Manning, P. Raghavan, and H. Schütze. 2008. *Introduction to Information Retrieval.* Cambridge University Press.

J. Pustejovsky, P. Hanks, R. Saurí, A. See, R.Gaizauskas, A. Setzer, D. Radev, B. Sundheim, D. Day, L. Ferro, and M. Lazo. 2003. The TIMEBANK corpus. *Corpus Linguistics*, pages 647–656.

TDT. 2004. TDT 2004: Annotation Manual Version 1.2. URL: `http://projects.ldc.upenn.edu/TDT5/Annotation/TDT2004V1.2.pdf`.

R. Tobin, C. Grover, K. Byrne, J. Reid, and J. Walsh. 2010. Evaluation of georeferencing. In *Proceedings of GIR'10.*

# Tracking Information Flow between Primary and Secondary News Sources

**Will Radford** †‡ **Ben Hachey** ‡◇ **James R. Curran** †‡ **Maria Milosavljevic** ◇

School of Information Technologies† University of Sydney NSW 2006, Australia

Capital Markets CRC‡ 55 Harrington Street NSW 2000, Australia

Centre for Language Technology◇ Macquarie University NSW 2109, Australia

{wradford,james}@it.usyd.edu.au bhachey@cmcrc.com mariam@ics.mq.edu.au

## Abstract

Tracking information flow (IFLOW) is crucial to understanding the evolution of news stories. We present analysis and experiments for IFLOW between company announcements and newswire. Error analysis shows that many FPs are annotation errors and many FNs are due to coarse-grained document-level modelling. Experiments show that document meta-data features (e.g., category, length, timing) improve f-scores relative to upper bound by 23%.

## 1 Introduction

Tracking IFLOW between primary and secondary news sources provides insight into the contribution of participants and the role of sources. In finance, being alert and responsive to the nature of incoming information (e.g., novelty, price sensitivity) is central to successful trading (Zaheer and Zaheer, 1997). Traders need tools that flag price-sensitive information in a high-volume news feed. IFLOW is central to market surveillance, where unusual market activity (e.g., abnormal changes in trading price or volume) is linked to explanations in the information ecosystem (Milosavljevic et al., 2009).

In Australia, the Australian Securities Exchange (ASX) is the official syndicator of information that might affect a company's share price. Subsequently, a variety of secondary sources (e.g., news media, blogs, forums) repackage this information. We focus on the relationship between ASX company announcements and Reuters newswire, which filters and aggregates the key details from company announcements in near-real time.

## 2 Preliminary Results

We define IFLOW for capital markets as *a pair of documents where one repeats price-sensitive information from the other* (Radford et al., 2009). Pairs of ASX announcements and Reuters NewsScope Archive (RNA) stories covering the same company and released within a week of one another are manually annotated for presence or absence of IFLOW. These are used to train MEGAM (Daumé III, 2004) maximum entropy models for identifying IFLOW. Textual features include set-theoretic bags of word unigrams and bigrams over the document text and titles. Text, title and numeric token similarity scores (Metzler et al., 2005) provide a more general notion of similarity. The precision of numeric tokens is also represented. Counts of matched sentences and longest common sub-sequences capture longer units of reused text. Temporal features model the news cycle and news source responsiveness.

In development experiments (ten-fold cross validation, 30,249 ASX-RNA pairs), the system identifies IFLOW pairs at 89.5% f-score (Radford et al., 2009). In evaluation experiments (held-out test set, 1,621 ASX-RNA pairs), it achieves 76.6% f-score, significantly better than a text-only baseline (62.5%) and 10% less than the human upper bound (86.4%).

## 3 Error analysis

We engaged finance students (fourth-year or higher) to examine the 20 false positive (FP) errors with the highest IFLOW probabilities and the 20 false negative (FN) errors with the lowest IFLOW probabilities. Table 1 shows the resulting reassessment of the



*Proceedings of the NAACL HLT 2010 Workshop on Computational Linguistics in a World of Social Media*, pages 29–30, Los Angeles, California, June 2010. 

| Error | Correct | Incorrect | Ambiguous |
|---|---|---|---|
| FP | 4 (20%) | 15 (75%) | 1 (5%) |
| FN | 15 (75%) | 4 (20%) | 1 (5%) |

Table 1: Analysis of original annotation correctness.

original IFLOW annotation. For FPs, 75% were determined to have been incorrectly annotated as absent of IFLOW. This is not unexpected since IFLOW can be based on small details (e.g., '$2.45m profit') which are easily missed by annotators. This suggests that the system's actual precision may be higher than 90.9%. Mis-annotation is less common for FNs (20%). However, the proportion of DIGEST documents (those that report on multiple events) is much higher for FNs (75% compared to 30% for FPs). It is likely that legitimate textual similarity is lost in the noise of the irrelevant content.

## 4 Document Metadata Features

We add new features that take advantage of categorisation information in the source metadata. These include ASX tags for price sensitivity, ASX and RNA type tags and journalist revision comments embedded in RNA stories. These features model differences in IFLOW between document types (e.g., periodic reports are more likely to be reported than a dividend rate announcement). A feature representing the length of each ASX-RNA document is also included. We also add detail to the temporal features, including the day and month the announcement was released, as well as whether the announcement and story were released on the same day.

The metadata features lead to significantly better f-score in development experiments (Table 2). Subtractive feature analysis suggests that the document type and length features are effective ($p<0.05$) but the detailed temporal features are not. The revision comments are borderline ($p=0.051$). In Table 3, the metadata features improve the f-score by 23% over Radford et al. (2009) with respect to the upper bound, but the difference is not significant. The different precision-recall balance between experiments is consistent with Section 3.

## 5 Discussion and Future Work

We have developed a dataset for IFLOW in the context of financial text mining and demonstrated it is a feasible task using simple approaches. Future work will involve more advanced models. First, we will consider *sub-document* analysis, as suggested by the DIGEST FNs in the error analysis. This will also enable tools that highlight specific types of contribution (e.g., adding background context, novel analysis) within secondary sources. Furthermore, the wider IFLOW ecosystem includes other sources (e.g., bloggers, forum contributors) that should be analysed for leading and lagging indicators. Finally, a number of specific applications might serve as extrinsic evaluations of the IFLOW task. These include de-duplicating and aggregating information feeds and automatically attributing reported content to a source story.

| Features | P (%) | R (%) | F (%) |
|---|---|---|---|
| Radford et al. (2009) | 90.9 | 88.1 | 89.5 |
| + Metadata Features | **91.1** | ⋆⋆**89.3** | ⋆**90.2** |

Table 2: Precision (P), recall (R) and f-score (F) for development experiments (⋆: $p<0.05$, ⋆⋆: $p<0.01$).

| Features | P (%) | R (%) | F (%) |
|---|---|---|---|
| Text-only Baseline | 80.0 | 51.3 | 62.5 |
| Radford et al. (2009) | 84.5 | 70.1 | 76.6 |
| + Metadata Features | **86.3** | **72.6** | **78.9** |
| Human Upper Bound | 88.9 | 85.1 | 86.4 |

Table 3: P, R and F for evaluation experiments.

## References

Hal Daumé III. 2004. Notes on CG and LM-BFGS optimization of logistic regression. http://hal3.name/docs/daume04cg-bfgs.pdf.

Donald Metzler, Yaniv Bernstein, W. Bruce Croft, Alistair Moffat, and Justin Zobel. 2005. Similarity measures for tracking information flow. In *Proc. CIKM*, pages 517–524.

Maria Milosavljevic, Jean-Yves Delort, Ben Hachey, Bavani Arunasalam, Will Radford, and James R. Curran. 2009. Automating financial surveillance. In *Proceedings of the Workshop on Mining User-Generated Content for Security*.

Will Radford, Ben Hachey, James R. Curran, and Maria Milosavljevic. 2009. Tracking information flow in financial text. In *Proc. ALTA*, pages 11–19.

Akbar Zaheer and Srilata Zaheer. 1997. Catching the wave: alertness, responsiveness, and market influence in global electronic networks. *Management Science*, 43(11):1493–1509.

# Detecting controversies in Twitter: a first study

**Marco Pennacchiotti**
Yahoo! Labs
Sunnyvale, CA.
pennac@yahoo-inc.com

**Ana-Maria Popescu**
Yahoo! Labs
Sunnyvale, CA.
amp@yahoo-inc.com

Social media gives researchers a great opportunity to understand how the public feels and thinks about a variety of topics, from political issues to entertainment choices. While previous research has explored the likes and dislikes of audiences, we focus on a related but different task of detecting *controversies* involving popular entities, and understanding their causes. Intuitively, if people hotly debate an entity in a given period of time, there is a good chance of a controversy occurring. Consequently, we use Twitter data, boosted with knowledge extracted from the Web, as a starting approach: This paper introduces our task, an initial method and encouraging early results.

**Controversy Detection.** We focus on detecting controversies involving known entities in Twitter data. Let a $snapshot$ denote a triple $s = (e, \Delta t, tweets)$, where $e$ is an entity, $\Delta t$ is a time period and $tweets$ is the set of tweets from the target time period which refer to the target entity.[1]. Let $cont(s)$ denote the level of controversy associated with entity $e$ in the context of the snapshot $s$. Our task is as follows:

**Task.** Given an entity set $E$ and a snapshot set $S = \{(e, \Delta t, tweets) | e \in E\}$, compute the controversy level $cont(s)$ for each snapshot $s$ in $S$ and rank $S$ with respect to the resulting scores.

**Overall Solution.** Figure 1 gives an overview of our solution. We first select the set $B \subset S$, consisting of candidate snapshots that are likely to be controversial (*buzzy snapshots*). Then, for each snapshot in $B$, we compute the controversy score $cont$, by combining a *timely controversy* score ($tcont$) and a *historical controversy* score ($hcont$).

**Resources.** Our method uses a sentiment lexicon $SL$ (7590 terms) and a controversy lexicon $CL$ (750 terms). The *sentiment lexicon* is composed by augmenting the set of positive and negative polarity terms in OpinionFinder 1.5 [2] (e.g. 'love','wrong') with terms bootstrapped from a large set of user reviews. The *controversy lexicon* is compiled by mining controversial terms (e.g. 'trial', 'apology') from Wikipedia pages of people included in the Wikipedia *controversial topic* list.

**Algorithm 0.1:** CONTROVERSYDETECTION($S, Twitter$)

$select\ buzzy\ snapshots\ B \subset S$
**for** $s \in B$
$\begin{cases} tcont(s) = \alpha * MixSent(s) + (1-\alpha) * Controv(s)) \\ cont(s) = \beta * tcont(s) + (1-\beta) * hcont(s) \end{cases}$
$rank\ B\ on\ scores$
**return** $(B)$

Figure 1: Controversy Detection: Overview

**Selecting buzzy snapshots.** We make the simple assumption that if in a given time period, an entity is discussed more than in the recent past, then a controversy involving the entity is likely to occurr in that period. We model the intuition with the score:

$$b(s) = \frac{|tweets_s|}{(\sum_{i \in prev(s,N)} |tweets_i|)/N}$$

where $tweets_s$ is the set of tweets in the snapshot $s$; and $prev(s, N)$ is the set of snapshots referring to the same entity of $s$, in $N$ time periods previous to $s$. In our experiment, we use $N = 2$, i.e. we focus on two days before $s$. We retain as buzzy snapshots only those with $b(s) > 3.0$.

**Historical controversy score.** The $hcont$ score estimates the overall controversy level of an entity in Web data, independently of time. We consider $hcont$ our *baseline system*, to which we compare the Twitter-based models. The score is estimated on Web document data using the $CL$ lexicon as fol-

[1]We use 1-day as the time period $\Delta t$. E.g. *s=('Brad Pitt',12/11/2009,tweets)*

[2]J. Wiebe, T. Wilson, and C. Cardie. 2005. Annotating expressions of opinions and emotions in language. In Language Resources and Evaluation.



*Proceedings of the NAACL HLT 2010 Workshop on Computational Linguistics in a World of Social Media*, pages 31–32,
Los Angeles, California, June 2010. 

lows: $hcont(e) = k/|CL|$, where $k$ is the number of controversy terms $t'$ s.t. $PMI(e, t') > A$[3].

**Timely controversy score.** $tcont$ estimates the controversy of an entity by analyzing the discussion among Twitter's users in a given time period, i.e. in a given snapshot. It is a linear combination (tuned with $\alpha \in [0, 1]$) of two scores:
$MixSent(s)$: reflects the relative disagreement about the entity in the Twitter data from snapshot $s$. First, each of the $N$ tweets in $s$ is placed in one of the following sets: Positive ($Pos$), Negative ($Neg$), Neutral ($Neu$), based on the number of positive and negative $SL$ terms in the tweet. $MixSent$ is computed as:

$$MixSent(s) = \frac{Min(|Pos|, |Neg|)}{Max(|Pos|), |Neg|)} \times \frac{|Pos| + |Neg|}{N}$$

$Controv(s)$: this score reflects the presence of explicit controversy terms in tweets. It is computed as: $Controv(s) = |ctv|/N$, where $ctv$ is the set of tweets in $s$ which contain at least one controversy term from $CL$.

**Overall controversy score.** The overall score is a linear combination of the timely and historical scores: $cont(s) = \beta * tcont(s) + (1-\beta) * hcont(s)$, where $\beta \in [0, 1]$ is a parameter.

## Experimental Results

We evaluate our model on the task of ranking snapshots according to their controversy level. Our corpus is a large set of Twitter data from Jul-2009 to Feb-2010. The set of entities $E$ is composed of 104,713 celebrity names scraped from Wikipedia for the Actor, Athlete, Politician and Musician categories. The overall size of $S$ amounts to 661,226 (we consider only snapshots with a minimum of 10 tweets). The number of buzzy snapshots in $B$ is 30,451. For evaluation, we use a **gold standard** of 120 snapshots randomly sampled from $B$, and manually annotated as controversial or not-controversial by two expert annotators (detailed guidelines will be presented at the workshop). Kappa-agreement between the annotators, estimated on a subset of 20 snapshots, is 0.89 ('almost perfect' agreement). We experiment with different $\alpha$ and $\beta$ values, as reported in Table 1, in order to discern the value of final score components. We use *Average Precision* (AP), and the *area under the ROC curve* (AROC) as our evaluation measures.

| Model | $\alpha$ | $\beta$ | AP | AROC |
|---|---|---|---|---|
| hcont (baseline) | 0.0 | 0.0 | 0.614 | 0.581 |
| tcont-MixSent | 1.0 | 1.0 | 0.651 | 0.642 |
| tcont-Controv | 0.0 | 1.0 | 0.614 | 0.611 |
| tcont-combined | 0.5 | 1.0 | 0.637 | 0.642 |
| cont | 0.5 | 0.5 | 0.628 | 0.646 |
| cont | 0.8 | 0.8 | 0.643 | 0.642 |
| cont | 1.0 | 0.5 | **0.660** | **0.662** |

Table 1: Controversial Snapshot Detection: results over different model parametrizations

The results in Table 1 show that all Twitter-based models perform better than the Web-based baseline. The most effective basic model is $MixSent$, suggesting that the presence of mixed polarity sentiment terms in a snapshot is a good indicator of controversy. For example, 'Claudia Jordan' appears in a snapshot with a mix of positive and negative terms -in a debate about a red carpet appearance- but the $hcont$ and $Controv$ scores are low as there is no record of historical controversy or explicit controversy terms in the target tweets. Best overall performance is achieved by a mixed model combining the $hcont$ and the $MixSent$ score (last row in Table label 1). There are indeed cases in which the evidence from $MixSent$ is not enough - e.g., a snapshot discussing 'Jesse Jackson' 's appearance on a tv show lacks common positive or negative terms, but reflects users' confusion nevertheless; however, 'Jesse Jackson' has a high historical controversy score, which leads our combined model to correctly assign a high controversy score to the snapshot. Interestingly, most controversies in the gold standard refer to *micro-events* (e.g., tv show, award show or athletic event appearances), rather than more traditional controversial events found in news streams (e.g., speeches about climate change, controversial movie releases, etc.); this further strengthens the case that Twitter is a complementary information source wrt news corpora.

We plan to follow up on this very preliminary investigation by improving our Twitter-based sentiment detection, incorporating blog and news data and generalizing our controversy model (e.g., discovering the 'what' and the 'why' of a controversy, and tracking common controversial behaviors of entities over time).

[3]PMI is computed based on the co-occurrences of entities and terms in Web documents; here we use $A = 2$.

# Author Index